TABLE OF CONTENTS

LIST OF FIGURES

THIS PAGE INTENTIONALLY LEFT BLANK

LIST OF TABLES

THIS PAGE INTENTIONALLY LEFT BLANK

ACKNOWLEDGMENTS

We would like to thank the many people who have personally and professionally inspired us in the pursuit of this thesis. To our advisors, Professors Doug Borer and George Lober, and our second reader, Norm Gardner, we are thankful for your comments, advice, and experience that helped shape this study. Your direct, yet patient approach kept us on track. To our editor, Mrs. Elizabeth Robinson, thank you for your help. Your skills were much needed and appreciated. To LtGen Wurster, Professor Joseph Nye, Ms. Gracia Burnham, Special Operations Command, Pacific (SOCPAC) staff, and our friends in the Philippine military and government, we are deeply appreciative of your time and insight into this important, yet complex issue. To our colleagues and classmates, thank you for sharing your thoughts and experiences with us. Lastly, to our families and to our spouses, Miso Smith, Jeffrey Stroh, and Mildred Williams we are so very blessed to have your loving and selfless support in all that we do.

THIS PAGE INTENTIONALLY LEFT BLANK

LIST OF ABBREVIATIONS AND ACRONYMS

AFP	Armed Forces of the Philippines
AQ	Al Qaeda
ARMM	Autonomous Region of Muslim Mindanao
ARSOF	Army Special Operations Forces
ASG	Abu Sayyaf Group
BMA	Bangsa Moro Army
CAFGU	Citizens Armed Forces Geographic Units
CAT	Civil Affairs Team
COIN	Counterinsurgency
GRP	Government of the Republic of Philippines
IMET	International Military Education and Training
JI	Jemaah Islamiya
JTF	Joint Task Force
MILF	Moro Islamic Liberation Front
MIM	Muslim Independent Movement
MLSA	Mutual Logistics Support Agreement
MNLF	Moro National Liberation Front
NoöPower	Nye's concept of Soft Power combined with the notion of Noöpolitik
NoöStrategy	Elements of Noöpolitik incorporated in strategic planning
ODA	Operational Detachment - A
OEF	Operation Enduring Freedom
OEF-P	Operation Enduring Freedom – Philippines
PACOM	Pacific Command
PSYOP	Psychological Operations
SF	Special Forces
SOCOM	Special Operations Command
SOCPAC	Special Operations Command – Pacific
VFA	Visiting Forces Agreement
VFACOM	Philippine Presidential Commission on the Visiting Forces

THIS PAGE INTENTIONALLY LEFT BLANK

I.   INTRODUCTION

A.   BACKGROUND

Terrorist organizations continue to use the southern Philippines as a sanctuary for training and recruitment. Mindanao, in particular, is a fertile land for terrorist organizations such as the Jemaah Islamiya (JI) and Abu Sayyaf Group (ASG). Members of JI, responsible for the 2002 Bali bombing, are thought to be hiding in Mindanao. Meanwhile, members of the ASG, responsible for the kidnapping of three American citizens, including missionary couple Martin and Gracia Burnham, and the subsequent deaths of two of the three American hostages, continue to elude Philippine authorities despite joint U.S. – Philippine efforts and ongoing operations to track them down.

Aside from the JI and ASG, Mindanao has experienced its share of violence from renegade members of the Muslim separatist group, the Moro Islamic Liberation Front (MILF). The MILF has publicly rejected the jihad against the United States and condemned the attack on 9/11, but the organization has social ties with and covertly supports the JI. In particular, the MILF supported the thirteen-member group of JI operatives arrested early in 2002 in Singapore while plotting to bomb western Embassies.[1] In spite of the fact that a handful of terrorists have been brought to justice, these terrorist organizations continue to threaten the people and stability of the region.

The U.S. has dedicated financial aid, military training and equipment to help fortify the Philippine government's capabilities to stabilize the region through efforts such as denying sanctuary to terrorist groups, isolating them from their support base, and capturing or killing terrorist members. Since 2002, the Armed Forces of the Philippines (AFP) and the U.S. military have combined efforts to restore some level of peace and normalcy to both Muslims and Christians in the southern Philippines. These cooperative actions, through training in

---

[1] Mike Millard, Jihad in Paradise: Islam and Politics in Southeast Asia (New York: M.E. Sharpe, Inc., 2004), 27.

unconventional warfare, have affected ASG's ability to conduct activities on the island of Basilan and marginalized their support base. Yet attaining a successful long-term counterinsurgency effort in Mindanao has proven more difficult. This thesis identifies what needs to be done, how, and by whom. A closer examination of both the possible flaws in the U.S.'s current counterinsurgency strategy and the interaction between the government of the Philippines and its citizens may lead to the development of a more effective approach to dealing with radical Islamic movement in the southern Philippines.

B.   RELEVANCY

Recent violent attacks in Mindanao, including the July 2007 beheading of thirteen members of the AFP and the deliberate car bombing of the Philippine Congressional building in November 2007, which resulted in two dead and nine injured, suggest that the seeds of terror are far from dormant domestically and internationally.[2] However, this resurgence of violence is not a new condition. Radical Filipino groups connected to other extremist elements have long used violence as a tool to further their cause.

For example, consider the October 2001 case of Father Rohan Al-Ghozi, code named "Mike," a key Al Qaeda operative in Southeast Asia. According to Rohan Gunaratna, an Islamic terrorism expert, Al-Ghozi was a Javanese who worked as an explosives trainer in Afghanistan and was JI's number one operative in Southeast Asia.[3] Al-Ghozi was also the connection between the local groups and Al Qaeda, according to former CNN correspondent Maria Ressa.[4] Ressa described Al-Ghozi as "an empowered local guy," adding that because Al-Ghozi had extensive training, knew the region and could speak all

---

[2] Delon Porcalla, *"2 Dead in the Batasan blast: Akbar, Driver Killed, and 12 hurt"*, The Philippine Star, 14 November 2007, Vol. XXII, No. 109, sec. A.

[3] "Al Qaeda Suspect Sentenced: 12 Years in Philippines Prison for Indonesian Man with Terror Links" *CBS News,* April 18, 2002, http://www.cbsnews.com/stories/2002/04/18/terror/main506549.shtml, (Accessed July 21, 2008).

[4] Former CNN correspondent Maria Ressa has been appointed Head of News and Current Affairs at ABS-CBN. Ressa was CNN's investigative reporter in Asia and was the bureau chief for its Southeast Asia operations.

the languages, he could blend into the local scene. "He could be a hand, he could be planner," Ressa stated. "He is that nexus, and part of the reason he was so important was that he connected different cells all across the region."[5]

Al-Ghozi was not only a master planner but he was an expert in explosives. Only a year earlier, he had attacked four targets in Manila, including an attack on commuter trains in which twenty-two people were killed. Al-Ghozi was arrested in the Philippines on 15 January 2002, a few hours before he was to flee the country for Bangkok for an arranged meeting with Riduan Isamuddin and other Al Qaeda and JI operatives. In April 2002, he pleaded guilty to charges of possession of illegal explosives, and was sentenced to 12 years in jail.[6]

While in custody, he revealed to investigators the location in General Santos City in Mindanao of a hidden stash of explosives and materials that could have easily produced hundreds of lethal bombs. Al-Ghozi confessed that he had provided the explosives used in the Rizal Day Bombings, and had been planning to use the remaining explosives to attack embassies in Singapore and Indonesia.

On 14 July 2003, Al-Ghozi escaped from a high security facility in Manila, along with two other prisoners suspected of belonging to the ASG. During the nationwide hunt for these fugitives, Al-Ghozi was killed in a police shootout in Mindanao when he attempted to ram a military roadblock. Soldiers shot Al-Ghozi as he tried to detonate a hand grenade; he died on the way to a nearby clinic.[7]

Al Ghozi's notorious emergence provides insight into the new generation of terrorists throughout Southeast Asia and their connection to a larger network of trained operatives and sympathizers. Al-Ghozi's testimony also revealed the ability of these radicals to move quickly between parts of the world that are poorly governed and inadequately policed where they can find sanctuary. Given the

---

[5] Maria Ressa, "Passport to Terrorism" *CBS News Online Indepth,* http://www.cbc.ca/news/background/jabarah, (Accessed on June 11, 2007).

[6] Global Security, www.globalsecurity.org/security/profiles/fathur_rahman_al-ghozi.htm (Accessed on July 21, 2008).

[7] Maria Ressa, "Passport to Terrorism" *CBS News Online Indepth,* http://www.cbc.ca/news/background/jabarah, (Accessed on June 11, 2007).

Philippines current political and security environment, radical groups are attracted to Mindanao where they can train and recruit more members. Confronting this regional issue as part of the global fight is a challenge in itself. To compound the issue, there remain inconsistencies in the U.S. counterinsurgency operations, the Philippine government's strategy in dealing with terrorism, and the Philippine government's efforts in dealing with its citizens. Perhaps the inconsistencies can be partly attributed to their joint COIN effort, which addresses the immediate threat while arguably providing limited staying power. Furthermore, militant Islamic groups within the Philippines have continued to destabilize peace negotiations between Muslims and Christians in Mindanao. Ongoing terrorist activity threatens the safety of the general population throughout the country and disrupts any chance of prosperity for all ethnicities. This thesis seeks to offer alternative approaches to this persistent problem.

C.   RESEARCH QUESTIONS

Recent studies have examined the rising threat in the Philippines, and they do offer some useful insight into a range of approaches, from U.S.– Philippine theater security cooperation programs to AFP preemptive military actions. However, while these various strategies and approaches have enjoyed some level of success, they also suffer from limited effectiveness in that they produce short-term results. Therefore, this thesis will attempt to answer the following questions:

1. What are the conditions contributing to the grievances in Mindanao and the subsequent spread of Islamic extremism there?
2. What are the linkages between operational and strategic successes on Basilan that have enabled successful COIN there?
3. Is the Basilan model applicable to other COIN operations in Mindanao as well as other conflicts in the world?
4. How can soft power and noöpolitik be implemented to reduce terrorist recruitment?

D. METHODOLOGY

There is an extensive body of research on the history of militant Islam in Southeast Asia, which examines the extent of the militant threat to the region. The research examines the links between regional and transnational networks. Much of the strength of these scholarly works lies in their analyses of the networks that recruit new members into existing organizations and new cells. Most of these studies are relevant in establishing the background of terrorist groups examined in this study. However, many of them minimize the threat of militant Islam by describing these radicals merely as groups of bandits or thugs engaged in local criminal activity.

This thesis presents a theoretical, informative and comparative case analysis of Basilan and Mindanao that studies the broad application of both hard and soft power. Specifically, the study analyzes both the impact of hard power as it is applied in Basilan and the subsequent soft power effects in Mindanao, using Nye and Arquilla's definitions of soft power and noöpolitik.[8] These effects will be quantitatively measured by considering the independent variables of U.S. and Philippine policy and best practices used in Operation Enduring Freedom-Philippines (OEF-P) to determine their impact on the dependent variables of public opinion and popular support of the Philippine government. By conducting a mixed method study using historical studies, interviews, surveys, and poll analysis, this thesis seeks to provide a well-researched analysis of the possibilities of an effective deterrence strategy which will yield long-term results.

This thesis explores the current U.S. counterinsurgency strategy by recognizing effective practices and identifying shortfalls in the current approach. Once such gaps have been located, attempts will be made to propose an

---

[8] Joseph Nye, a professor at Harvard and International Relations expert, coined the term "Soft Power" in the late 1980s. John Arquilla, a professor at NPS and an unconventional warfare expert, along with David Ronfeldt, furthers the concept of Soft Power by advancing the idea of Noöpolitik.

alternative strategy by applying elements of soft power, as defined by Nye,[9] as well as noöpolitik, as defined by Arquilla and Ronfeldt

Joseph Nye, a recognized expert in the field of International Relations, has written extensively on soft power.[11] He suggests that the U.S. should use its power, specifically soft power, to attract or entice those who, through their values and culture, actively or passively support terrorism.

Arquilla and Ronfeldt's article, "The Promise of Noöpolitik," offers a new perspective on a "revolution in diplomatic affairs," which defines the traditional realpolitik in relation to the more contemporary noöpolitik.[12] Too heavy a reliance on hard power, or what is more commonly known as military power, impacts a nation's ability to employ noöpolitik, which is defined as an approach or art of governing that emphasizes the role of information in expressing ideas, values, norms, and ethics.

By examining OEF-P through soft power and noöpolitik, the research will analyze U.S. and Philippine counterinsurgency strategy and offer a long-term sustainable course of action that will diminish future radical Islamic threats by reducing recruitment. A key aspect in deterring terrorist recruitment is to identify the underlying conditions that promote discontent that make people vulnerable to recruitment. It is clear that the people of Mindanao have suffered from a lack of adequate social, economic, and educational programs. Socioeconomic factors are important in predicting the potential for terrorist recruitment, but these are not the only conditions. These factors, combined with poor governance have contributed to the instability there. Understanding that the U.S. and Philippine

---

[9] Joseph Nye, *Soft Power* (New York: Public Affairs, 2004).

[10] John Arquilla and David Ronfeldt, "The Promise of Noöpolitik" *First Monday*, http://www.firstmonday.org/issues/issue12_8/ronfeldt/index.html. (Accessed on February 17, 2008).

[11] Joseph S. Nye, Jr. served as Chairman of the National Intelligence Council and an Assistant Secretary of Defense in the Clinton Administration.

[12] David Ronfeldt is a senior political scientist at the RAND Corporation. John Arquilla is a Professor of Defense Analysis at the Naval Postgraduate School. In "The Promise of Noöpolitik," they share their views that the power of "the story" is at stake in the worldwide war of ideas.

governments may lack credibility with the people of Mindanao, this thesis will also examine the best practices and methods to connect the Philippine people to their government.

E.   ORGANIZATION

Chapter II describes the differences between the terms hard power and soft power, and will discuss the importance of soft power in minimizing the effects of terrorism within the Philippines. The theoretical concepts of Nye, Ronfeldt, and Arquilla are used in support of this thesis.

Chapter III provides a historical overview of events that have led to the spread of terrorism in the Philippines. Chapter III also addresses some of the current issues and tensions that are straining the fabric of the country.

Chapter IV discusses both pre- and post-9/11 counterinsurgency operations on the southern island of Basilan and throughout affected terrorist areas in Central Mindanao. Interviews with the Joint Task Force commanders of 510, select Special Operations Detachment (ODA) and Civil Affairs Team (CAT) members present a unique U.S. military perspective on OEF-P. The chapter also discusses how political constraints may have contributed to OEF-P's success.

Chapter V presents the counterinsurgency struggle from the Filipino perspective. Interviews with key AFP and government officials provide a more complete picture of the threat to stability within the country; they also help outsiders to understand the Philippine cultural and social dilemmas that challenge counterinsurgency operations.

Chapter VI proposes a method to validate or invalidate the applicability of theoretical approaches. It also offers suggestions for the operational application of soft power, and provides further recommendations based on the results of this study.

F.   SIGNIFICANT WORKS

A major source for this study is *Soft Power: The Means to Success in World Politics,* by Joseph S. Nye, Jr.[13] Nye coined the term "Soft Power." His work provides a solid understanding of the meaning of "Soft Power" and its relevance to the War on Terror, and provides the conceptual framework for this study.

Noöpolitik is an approach to diplomacy and strategy for the information age that emphasizes the shaping and sharing of ideas, values norms, laws, and ethics through "Soft Power."[14]

Another significant book utilized for this thesis is *Militant Islam in Southeast Asia* by Zachary Abuza.[15] Abuza has researched and written extensively on the militant Islamic movement. This book gives historical context to the conditions that allowed militant Islam to grow in Southeast Asia.

"Deterrence and Influence in Counterterrorism", a RAND study by Paul K. Davis and Brian Michael Jenkins, offers insight into deterrence and counterterrorism.[16] This study provides useful information about deep-rooted problems with deterrence strategies, and offers options for dealing with terrorists and their supporters.

The theoretical counterinsurgency models of the "Mystic Diamond" by Gordon McCormick and "COIN Best Practices" by Kalev Sepp provide a framework for analyzing OEF-P operational execution and what is commonly referred to as an unconventional approach. The "Mystic Diamond" is a dynamic model that considers the interaction between the state or host

---

[13] Joseph Nye, *Soft Power* (New York: Public Affairs, 2004).

[14] John Arquilla and David Ronfeldt, "The Promise of Noöpolitik" *First Monday,* http://www.firstmonday.org/issues/issue12_8/ronfeldt/index.html. (Accessed on February 17, 2008).

[15] Zachary Abuza. *Militant Islam in Southeast Asia* (Boulder, Lynne Rienner Publishers, 2003)

[16]Paul K. Davis and Brian Michael Jenkins "Deterrence and Influence in Counterterrorism" (Santa Monica, RAND Corporation, 2002), http://www.rand.org/pubs/monograph_reports/MR1619. (Accessed on February 17, 2008).

nation government, the insurgent or terrorist group, the general public, and the international actors or sponsors.[17] "COIN Best Practices" historically analyzes the nature and staying power of terrorist organizations over time in various cultural, political, and geographical settings.[18]

---

[17] Gordon McCormick is the Department Chair for Defense Analysis at the Naval Postgraduate School. His "Mystic Diamond" approach is a theoretical illustration that laid the conceptual groundwork incorporated in counterinsurgency strategy of OEF-P, which was written about by Colonel Gregory Wilson in, *Anatomy of a Successful COIN Operations: OEF-Philippines and the Indirect Approach, p. 4*

[18] Kalev Sepp is an associate professor in Defense Analysis at the Naval Postgraduate School. His theoretical application of "Counterinsurgency Best Practices" is an article in Military Review May-June 2005.

THIS PAGE INTENTIONALLY LEFT BLANK

II.   SOFT, HARD AND NOÖPOWER

Grand strategy looks beyond the war to the subsequent peace. It should not only combine the various instruments of power, but so regulate their use as to avoid damage to the future state of peace[19]

B.H. Liddell Hart

The U.S. is unquestionably the most powerful country in the world, with great capabilities and abundant resources. So, why is the U.S. finding it so difficult to win this war on terror? Why hasn't the kill and capture method stunted the recruitment of more operatives? How is it that seven years later, the U.S. is still struggling to find a way to dissuade youths from joining terrorist organizations? Can the U.S. apply its far reaching power to strategically influence other governments to join the global effort in this "long war." Although many experts have suggested a range of options in applying power to defeat terrorism, the reality is, there is a limit to power, especially in the case of military power against an unconventional foe.

As the U.S. leads the world in the current war, its use of military power has dominated the news. Domestic and international media routinely broadcast bombings of villages, raids on homes, and harsh interrogation tactics that continue to paint a picture of the U.S. as a world bully. This has negatively affected the U.S.'s image and jeopardized long-standing alliances. Countries that once supported the U.S. no longer allow access to their ports, airstrips, or airspaces, while other countries fan the flame of anti-Americanism.

The U.S.'s tarnished image and decline of influence abroad has allowed its enemies to gain ground—ground that provides a space for terrorists to operate, train, and recruit support. Each new conflict between the U.S. and its enemies fuels radical groups. Additionally, the Global War on Terror is perceived as a war against Islam, which further alienates segments of the Muslim population and marginalizes other Muslim groups in Christian dominated

---

[19] Basil Liddell Hart, *Strategy* (New York: Penguin Group, 1991), 322.

societies. Within this marginalized Muslim population, terrorist groups find recruits to serve a range of positions from active participants to passive supporters. Similar to AQ, radical Islamic groups such as the ASG and JI rely on the full span of support of the people in order to sustain and expand their cause.

In 2002, the U.S. and Philippine governments entered a bilateral agreement to conduct military training in southern Philippines. As part of Operation Enduring Freedom – Philippines, the U.S. military is strengthening the Armed Forces of the Philippines through counterinsurgency training to separate the people from the radical groups. The training includes a broad net of activities from civic action projects to direct action drills. Despite the relative success of OEF-P in defeating the ASG, the U.S. and Philippine governments have been criticized over their use of the military to what is largely viewed as a political problem, while others speculate whether this short-term military exchange will yield a long-term success. With this in mind, a better understanding of power and the balance between soft and hard power is essential in order to address the issue of counterinsurgency and counter-terrorism in the southern Philippines.

A.   POWER DEFINED

To appreciate the impact of power, one must first understand the concept of power in general. In broad terms, power is the ability to influence actions in order to achieve a desired outcome. In other words, "Practical politicians and ordinary people often simply define power as the possession of capabilities or resources that can influence outcomes."[20] Given this definition, a country such as the U.S., with a large military and an abundance of natural resources, is powerful. However, this definition is flawed in that it does not account for undesired outcomes. For example, the U.S. is a powerful nation, yet it could not prevent the actions of violent extremist organizations from taking the American Embassy in Tehran in 1979, bombing of the American Embassy and Marine Corps barracks in Beirut, Lebanon in1983, destroying Pan Am Flight 102 over

---

[20] Joseph S. Nye Jr. "The Benefits of Soft Power," August 2, 2004: http://hbswk.hbs.edu/archieve/4290.html// (Accessed on January 20, 2008).

Lockerbie, Scotland in 1988, bombing the World Trade Center in 1993, bombing the Khobar Towers military housing in Dhahran in 1996, bombing the African embassy in 1998, bombing the USS Cole in 2000, or attacking the U.S. on 9/11.

Despite the shortfall in defining power by the capability to influence actions, it is understandable why defining power in terms of resources is preferred. It's easy to measure and quantify. As Nye stated, "Measuring power in terms of resources is imperfect but useful shorthand. It is equally important to understand which resources provide the best basis for power behavior in a particular context."[21] In the context of counterinsurgency, the true measure of power is defined by influencing the people to no longer actively or passively supports radical groups. In Nye's own words, "power is the ability to influence others to get what you want, and there are ultimately three main ways for a nation to achieve power: by using or threatening force; by inducing compliance with rewards; or by using "soft power"—attracting followers and co-opting them."[22]

Deploying power in appropriate ways by considering the strengths of the different instruments of power to include noöpolitik is more challenging that it appears on the surface. For instance, hard and soft power sometimes reinforce and sometimes interfere with each other. "A leader who courts popularity may be loath to exercise hard power when he should, but a leader who throws his weight around without regard to the effects on his soft power may find others placing obstacles in the way of his hard power."[23] Although the two forms of power have been misunderstood, the distinctions between them are important and relevant to the U.S.'s ability to win the war on terror in general, and its ability to affect the stability of Mindanao in particular.

---

[21] Joseph S. Nye Jr. "The Benefits of Soft Power," August 2, 2004: http://hbswk.hbs.edu/archieve/4290.html// (Accessed on January 20, 2008).

[22] Joseph S. Nye Jr. "The Benefits of Soft Power," August 2, 2004: http://hbswk.hbs.edu/archieve/4290.html// (Accessed on January 20, 2008).

[23] Joseph S. Nye Jr., "The Benefits of Soft Power," August 2, 2004: http://hbswk.hbs.edu/archieve/4290.html// (Accessed on January 20, 2008).

B.   HARD POWER

Hard power, as the term suggests, often involves aggression and is associated with the use of military force. In terms of political tools, hard power is a form of political power that lies on one end of the spectrum. According to Nye, "hard power is a nation's ability to coerce or induce another nation into a desired action through the use of threats or rewards. It can involve both the use of force or aggression through military action and the use of economic means through incentives."[24] Typically, hard power is categorized by coercion and inducements. Coercion is the threat or the use of military force, as well as the enforcement of economic sanctions. It is often referred to as the "stick." Inducement is the ability to influence a desired behavior through a reward or an incentive. It is often referred to as the "carrot."[25]

1.   Limits of Hard Power

Extensive reliance on hard power presents a number of potential pitfalls for U.S. policy. Military force can be used inappropriately, hindering the U.S. in achieving its national objectives and eroding public support. Military force can also undermine existing alliances and lead to the creation of hostile coalitions. Yet another criticism of hard power is that once it ends, the affected state or organization can and often does revert back to its original behavior. Furthermore, it requires clearly articulated and understood demands and continuous assessments.

Perhaps the most significant drawback to hard power is the cost. The Congressional Budget Office estimates that, to date, "$440 billon has been spent fighting the war on terror. Funding for the U.S. operations in Iraq and Afghanistan have averaged about $93 billion a year from 2003 – 2005 and are estimated at $171 billion for 2007. Current estimates expect the cost to continue

---

[24] Joseph S. Nye Jr. "The Benefits of Soft Power," August 2, 2004: http://hbswk.hbs.edu/archieve/4290.html// (Accessed on January 20, 2008).

[25] Joseph S. Nye Jr. "The Benefits of Soft Power," August 2, 2004: http://hbswk.hbs.edu/archieve/4290.html// (Accessed on January 20, 2008).

to rise, with $193 billion expected for 2008."[26] What is not so widely discussed by supporters of the war is the real cost of military force, and the consequences paid for that choice. Even more sobering is the human toll: "more than 3,800 U.S. service members have died to date, and more than 28,000 have been wounded."[27]

Proponents and critics both acknowledge that the instruments of hard power, typically the Department of Defense, are better funded, larger, and more influential than the other instruments of soft power, typically the Department of State. The reality is that soft power institutions are often subordinate to and lack the clout of their hard power counterparts. Still, critics claim that the use of hard power in the war on terror has done little to change a deteriorating situation. In fact, much of the hostility against U.S. military action has ignited factors that contribute to recruiting more members and supporters of violent extremist organizations. A different political strategy may have achieved more without incurring such a considerable cost. Had the U.S. applied less force and more finesse, it is possible that scarce resources could have been used in ways that are more judicious, lives could have been spared, and the U.S. could have seen a better return on its investment.

C.   SOFT POWER

Joseph Nye, who coined the phrase "soft power," explains that, "[soft power] is the ability to get what you want through attraction rather than coercion or payments. It arises from the attractiveness of a country's culture, political ideals, and policies."[28] In other words, soft power is the ability to attract. This should not be confused with the widely used "carrots and sticks" analogy. Rather, it is meant to further define soft power as a separate form of power

---

[26] Reuters, "U.S. War Costs in Iraq Up – Budget Report", January 23, 2008: http://www.reuters.com/article/asiaCrisis/idUSN23650654 (Accessed on January 20, 2008).

[27] "What Does Iraq Cost? Even More Than You Think", November 18, 2007: http://www.washingtonpost.com/wp-dyn/content/article/2007/11/16/AR2007111600865.html (Accessed on January 20, 2008).

[28] Joseph S. Nye Jr., *Soft Power: The Means to Success in World Politics* (Public Affairs: New York, 2004), 28.

outside of inducements (carrots) or coercion (sticks). Soft power is simply another form of power to be used in conjunction with or as an alternative option to hard power. Nye offers that, "When a country can induce others to follow by employing soft power, it saves a lot of carrots and sticks."[29]

Soft power seeks to influence or persuade through the power of attraction. However, soft power is not the same as influence, which can rest on the hard power of threats or payments. Nye explains that, "soft power involves the ability to move people by argument, and the ability to attract, which often leads to acquiescence. Simply put, in behavioral terms, soft power is attractive power. Soft power resources are the assets that produce such attraction".[30]

To clarify soft power is to define what it is not. It is not economic inducement in the form of aid, and it is not military coercion in the form of kinetic action. Economic and military factors can play a role in soft power; however, soft power exerts its influence through the appeal of an attractive force.

Another way that hard and soft power differ is in the way they are employed. Hard power relies on threats, sanctions, and restrictions that are aimed at changing behavior by making a state behave in a way that it would not otherwise behave. On the other hand, soft power is at play if a state chooses to act in a manner that is in concert with its desire to emulate another state, or because of its attraction to that other state's values.

In the past, the U.S.'s soft power was effective and successful in many parts of the world. For example, Radio Free Europe broadcasts to communist Eastern Europe attracted many listeners to include many young people in the former Soviet Union. Radio Free Europe provided an alternative to the state controlled information and provided people with another side of the story which appealed to many within the Iron Curtain.[31] Although many listeners were drawn

---

[29] Joseph S. Nye Jr., *Soft Power: The Means to Success in World Politics* (Public Affairs: New York, 2004), 28.

[30] Ibid.

[31] Radio Free Europe www.rferl.org/content/article/1073305.html (accessed on September 28, 2008).

to the station to hear western music, they also received messages of American values and policies. To many academics, this effort was not so much a war against communism but rather a war against ideas which was largely won by America's soft power.

In the current war on terror, Nye's theory of soft power is helpful in addressing questions often raised about U.S. strategy. For instance, to what extent can the U.S. tackle this global issue alone while bypassing unwilling or incapable allies to defeat terrorism? In the case of Syria, prior to 9/11 the Syrian leadership provided intelligence to the U.S. despite a history of strained political relations. Today, the United States' relations with Syria are even more strained. Nye argues that rather than being less dependent on countries like Syria, America will become increasingly dependent on other nations to help defeat terrorism within the borders of those countries.

Although the need to partner with other nations has increased, American soft power continues to decline. Countries such as Britain and Spain, with whom the U.S. has shared a strong relationship, are backing away from U.S. policies. Meanwhile, polls capture a dramatic downturn of popular opinion in Islamic countries. Nye further supports this decline in American soft power by stating that, "In Indonesia, the world's largest Islamic nation, three quarters of the public said they had a favorable opinion of the United States in 2000, but within three years that fraction had shrunk to 15 percent."[32] Yet according to Nye, "the cooperation of these countries is essential if the United States and its allies are to succeed in a long-term struggle against terrorism."[33]

The Philippines is an example of this type of government cooperation with which the U.S. seeks to partner. While the U.S. is unrivaled militarily, it cannot monitor every part of the world, nor should it act alone. Appealing to common

---

[32] Joseph Nye, *"Politics in an information age is not only about whose military wins but whose story wins",* February/March 2005, Boston Review, http://www.bostonreview.net/BR30.1/nye.html, (Accessed on April 27, 2008).

[33] Joseph Nye, *"Politics in an information age is not only about whose military wins but whose story wins",* February/March 2005, Boston Review, http://www.bostonreview.net/BR30.1/nye.html, (Accessed on April 27, 2008).

interests, creating an attraction of shared values, and fostering a willingness to consult others can seems difficult; however, such tasks are necessary in order for the U.S. and other nations to pursue collectively desired outcomes such as the defeat of terrorist organizations.[34]

1.   Limits of Soft Power

Some skeptics object to the idea of soft power because they think of power narrowly in terms of commands or active control. In their view, imitation or attraction does not add up to power. Not all imitation or attraction exerts much power over policy outcomes, and neither does imitation always produce desirable outcomes. For instance, in reviewing Nye's 1990 work, *Bound to Lead: The Changing Nature of American Power*, Tysha Bohorquez makes the case that,

> A country has more soft power if its culture, values and institutions incite admiration and respect in other parts of the world. Diplomacy and a nation's standing in international bodies enable it to build alliances. Crucial to understanding Nye's concept of soft power is the importance of U.S. popular culture worldwide. From McDonald's to Hollywood movies, to the heavy U.S. flavor of the Internet, US culture has influence worldwide. Also relevant to the concept of soft power is the lure of the U.S. style of government widely esteemed for its freedoms and for the opportunity it offers immigrants. From these examples, Nye argues that, in both political and cultural terms, the U.S. has a great deal of soft power.[35]

But attraction is often an important source of influence. The skeptics who want to define power only as deliberate acts of command and control are ignoring an important aspect of power: the ability to achieve the outcomes desired without having to force people to change their behavior through threats or payments.

---

[34] Tysha Bohorquez, *"Soft Power -The Means to Success in World Politics"*, December 2005, UCLA International Institute, Tysha Bohorquez reviews Joseph Nye Jr.'s book on the importance of soft power, http://www.international.ucla.edu/article.asp?parentid=34734, (Accessed on April 27, 2008).

[35] Tysha Bohorquez, *"Soft Power -The Means to Success in World Politics"*, December 2005, UCLA International Institute, Tysha Bohorquez reviews Joseph Nye Jr.'s book on the importance of soft power, http://www.international.ucla.edu/article.asp?parentid=34734, (Accessed on April 27, 2008).

Perhaps the most significant limitation is based more on the uncertainty that shrouds this concept versus the capability itself. It's difficult to know exactly when soft power has had an impact and how it was achieved. At best, efforts to measure the effects of soft power are viewed as murky.

2. Arguments Against Soft Power

Despite the logic and usefulness of soft power theory, not everyone holds Nye's view. His critiques include David Frum, a former speechwriter to President George W. Bush, who is credited for coining the phrase "axis of evil," and Richard Perle, co-author with Frum of "An End to Evil: How to Win the War on Terror." Both Frum and Perle consider themselves "realists," advocating an aggressive approach to dealing with terrorists. They fully reject Nye's concept of soft power. In fact, Frum and Perle describe America's soft power approach in dealing with the budding problem of terrorism as weak-willed. Frum and Perle's vision of the world is black and white, defined by an "us against them" mentality. Bohorquez explains that, "while some argue that the U.S. government has overstepped its boundaries in the international arena, Perle and Frum claim that overthrowing the governments of Afghanistan and Iraq was not enough. Frum and Perle support the use of military action against North Korea, Iran, Syria, Libya and Saudi Arabia. To them, soft power is irrelevant for a country without military rivals."[36] This philosophy disregards the possibility of the co-existence of hard and soft power.

However, this rejection of soft power is not limited to Perle and Frum. According to Bohorquez, "[Former] Secretary of Defense Donald Rumsfeld is another skeptic of soft power. In fact, he admits to not even understanding the term, claiming that popularity is ephemeral and should not guide U.S. foreign policy. Rumsfeld asserts that America is strong enough to do as it wishes with or without the world's approval and should simply accept that others will envy and

---

[36] Tysha Bohorquez, *"Soft Power -The Means to Success in World Politics",* December 2005, UCLA International Institute, Tysha Bohorquez reviews Joseph Nye Jr.'s book on the importance of soft power, http://www.international.ucla.edu/article.asp?parentid=34734, (Accessed on April 27, 2008).

resent it. According to him, the world's only superpower does not need permanent allies; the issues should determine the coalitions, not vice-versa."[37]

D.   NOÖPOLITIK

Throughout the remainder of this thesis, the ideas of soft power and noöpolitik will serve as discussion points in the analysis of the Philippines, and more specifically U.S. government policy and U.S. military activities in the southern Philippines.

Nye's concept of soft power has served as the springboard for Arquilla and Ronfeldt's notion of noöpolitik, which is a "new approach to diplomacy and strategy."[38] More specifically, noöpolitik emphasizes the role of informational soft power as an important aspect of dealing with other organizations or nations. To clarify, Arquilla and Ronfeldt offer the following points to illustrate the differences of the more widely known realpolitik as compared to newer concept of noöpolitik:[39]

---

[37] Tysha Bohorquez, *"Soft Power -The Means to Success in World Politics"*, December 2005, UCLA International Institute, Tysha Bohorquez reviews Joseph Nye Jr.'s book on the importance of soft power, http://www.international.ucla.edu/article.asp?parentid=34734, (Accessed on 27 April 2008).

[38] John Arquilla and David Ronfeldt, "The Promise of Noöpolitik" *First Monday*, http://www.firstmonday.org/issues/issue12_8/ronfeldt/index.html. (Accessed on June 20, 2008).

[39] John Arquilla and David Ronfeldt, "The Promise of Noöpolitik" *First Monday*, http://www.firstmonday.org/issues/issue12_8/ronfeldt/index.html. (Accessed on June 20, 2008).

Table 1.   Realpolitik as compared to Noöpolitik

Contrast between realpolitik and noöpolitik.	
Realpolitik	**Noöpolitik**
States as the unit of analysis	Nodes, non–state actors
Primacy of hard power (resources, etc.)	Primacy of soft power
Power politics as zero–sum game	Win–win, lose–lose possible
System is anarchic, highly conflictual	Harmony of interests, cooperation
Alliance conditional (oriented to threat)	Ally webs vital to security
Primacy of national self–interest	Primacy of shared interests
Politics as unending quest for advantage	Explicitly seeking a *telos*
Ethos is amoral, if not immoral	Ethics crucially important
Behavior driven by threat and power	Common goals drive actors
Very guarded about information flows	Propensity for info–sharing
Balance of power as the "steady–state"	Balance of responsibilities
Power embedded in nation–states	Power in "global fabric"

Arquilla and Ronfeldt assert that soft power lacks operational clarity that requires further explanation in two ways:

1.   Soft and hard power require making a distinction between the two concepts which may or may not be based on what many consider to be non-military versus military power.

2.   Soft power is not always "good," and hard power is not always "bad." In fact, soft power can be wielded in shadowy ways by not-so-good people as in the case of Hitler or Osama Bin Laden.[40]

According to Arquilla and Ronfeldt, noöpolitik is "ultimately about whose story wins."[41] Noöpolitik is centered on ideas and how those ideas influence people to behave or act in deliberate ways. For example, America's principles and values of freedom, rule of law, respect for human rights, and humane treatment of individuals shape its domestic and foreign policies. Unfortunately,

---

[40] John Arquilla and David Ronfeldt, "The Promise of Noöpolitik" *First Monday*, http://www.firstmonday.org/issues/issue12_8/ronfeldt/index.html. (Accessed on February 17, 2008).

[41] John Arquilla and David Ronfeldt, "The Promise of Noöpolitik" *First Monday*, http://www.firstmonday.org/issues/issue12_8/ronfeldt/index.html. (Accessed on February 17, 2008).

the perception that the U.S.'s actions are contrary to these very principles and values has affected its soft power and noöpolitik.

E.   AMERICA'S SOFT POWER AND NOÖPOLITIK

The events of 9/11 opened a new chapter in history that reflects a growing love-hate relationship between the U.S. and the world. Polls and surveys indicate that a decline in American soft power is affecting its image and its ability to influence other nations. Dr. Steven Kull testified before a House Committee on Foreign Affairs on the results of a study on world public opinion taken in 26 countries. According to Kull, the BBC World Service/Globe Scan poll revealed that, "only 30 percent agree that the U.S. is having a mostly positive influence in the world while 51 percent say that the U.S. is having a mostly negative influence."[42] Even in Great Britain, which has good relations with the U.S., favorable opinions of the U.S. decreased from 83% in 1999/2000 to 56% in 2005/2006.[43]

---

[42] Steven Kull, "America's Image in the World," March 4, 2007, Testimony before House Committee on Foreign Affairs, Subcommittee on International Organizations, Human Rights, and Oversight: http://www.worldopinion.org (Accessed on January 21, 2008).

[43] . Steven Kull, "America's Image in the World," March 04, 2007, Testimony before House Committee on Foreign Affairs, Subcommittee on International Organizations, Human Rights, and Oversight: http://www.worldopinion.org (Accessed on January 21, 2008).

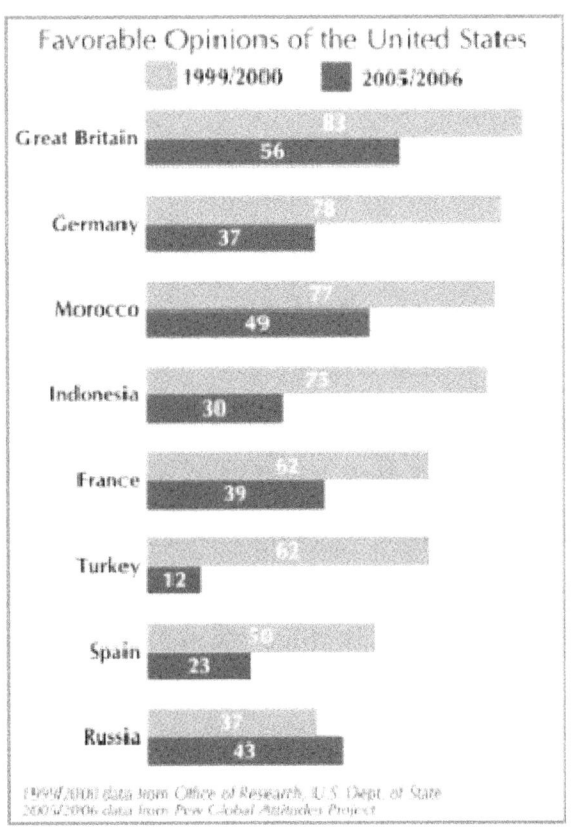

Figure 1. Opinions of the United States

It may appear that the primary reason for this decline in favorable opinion is the war in Iraq. However, although many countries did not support U.S. military action in March 2003, favorable opinions have continued to decline even four years after the invasion. The disparity between pre- and post -9/11 and the steady decline since 9/11 suggest that something deeper is at play.

According to a BBC poll, focus groups were questioned on their opinion of U.S. values, culture, and policies. The majority of countries support American values of human rights and democracy, and many still favor American culture, which they often experience through movies and music. Rather, the overwhelming numbers of complaints were based on the perception that the U.S. was not living up to its values, especially in foreign policy. Although many countries supported the removal of Saddam Hussein, they disagreed with the unilateral decision by the U.S. to invade Iraq. This was seen as hypocritical, in that the U.S. was promoting values that it did not practice.[44]

Large majorities of people agreed that "it was a good thing that the Americans knew what it was like to be vulnerable."[45] Startling results show that over 70% of non-Americans believe that the world would be improved if the U.S. faced a rival military power. These polls suggest that U.S. soft power is not only deteriorating, but that the projection of American hard power has detracted from America's ability to flex its soft power muscles.

Further research taken during A World Public Opinion Poll in October 2006 reveals that 75% of Americans felt that the most important lesson of September 11 was that the "U.S. needs to work more closely with other countries to fight terrorism, while 24% said that the U.S. needs to act on its own to fight terrorism."[46] The poll goes on to note that "Americans not only prefer a multilateral approach when dealing with terrorism, they also perceive that a unilateral approach can be counterproductive."[47] This is in line with a previous poll conducted in December 2004 by the Opinion Research Corporation that found 71% of respondents agreed with the statement that, "When the United States acts alone against terrorism, it makes itself a bigger target than when it cooperates with other nations in a coordinated crackdown on terrorism."[48] This may suggest why the U.S. and Philippine governments have experienced more success in their joint endeavors in the Philippines than the U.S. has in its efforts in Iraq and Afghanistan.

---

[44] Steven Kull, "America's Image in the World," March 04, 2007, Testimony before House Committee on Foreign Affairs, Subcommittee on International Organizations, Human Rights, and Oversight: http://www.worldpublicopinion.org (Accessed on June 20, 2008).

[45] Andrew Kohut and Bruce Stokes, *America Against the World: How We Are Different and Why We Are Disliked* (New York: Times Books, 2006). www.pewresearchcenter.org, (Accessed on January 28, 2008).

[46] "US Role in the World," http://www.americans-world.org/digest/overview/us_role/multilateralism.cfm, (Accessed on June 22, 2008).

[47] "US Role in the World," http://www.americans-world.org/digest/overview/us_role/multilateralism.cfm, (Accessed on June 22, 2008).

[48] "US Role in the World," http://www.americans-world.org/digest/overview/us_role/multilateralism.cfm, (Accessed on June 22, 2008).

Figure 2.   America's Role in the World[49]

The U.S. and Philippine governments implemented elements of noöpolitik in that they sought "primacy of shared interests"[50] in 2002 when the two countries agreed to conduct a joint military exercise, Balikatan 02-1, to strengthen the Armed Forces of the Philippines' counterinsurgency capabilities. Despite the challenging media environment of the Philippines where news is deliberately sensationalized to sell the story, the U.S. maintained its informational integrity by truthful reporting backed by its deeds. Furthermore, the U.S. military employed an active information strategy of getting the story out in front before its adversaries could distort or misrepresent the U.S. and Philippine governments' or militaries' intents or actions.

---

[49] "US Role in the World," http://www.americans-world.org/digest/overview/us_role/multilateralism.cfm, (Accessed on June 22, 2008).

[50] John Arquilla and David Ronfeldt, "The Promise of Noöpolitik" *First Monday,* http://www.firstmonday.org/issues/issue12_8/ronfeldt/index.html. (Accessed on June 20, 2008).

F. PHILIPPINE HARD POWER

The Philippines' history of employing hard power against insurgents is not exclusive to the Muslim Moros. Rather, the Philippine government and military lost public support during the Marcos regime when the military employed harsh tactics against civilians while confronting the growing communist and Muslim insurgencies. However, conventional tactics proved to be ineffective against the insurgents who garnered support from the people who were largely dissatisfied with their national government.

Meanwhile, the relationship between the Muslim Moros in the Sulu Archipelago and their Philippine government suffered. Sentiments of alienation were provoked by a perceived corrupt government and incapable military. The Moros seeking to defend their traditional practices of Islam, continued to face difficult social and economic situations that further aggravated their relationship with their Christian majority government. The Moro struggle is founded on a history of perceived marginalization and government policies that have not met the needs of the people. In many ways, the Moros felt that they were not legitimate members of the Philippines.

To complicate the delicate situation, in the early 1990s, the U.S. reduced its security assistance funding which further eroded the Philippine military operational capability. Yet, to further exacerbate the issue, charges of human rights abuses against the Philippine military and police have created more tension. Meanwhile, membership in the militant Islamic groups has not significantly decreased. In fact, alliances have formed between the Moro National Liberation Front (MNLF), MILF, and ASG, and are backed by international terrorist networks such as the JI. The general disaffection of the Moros towards their government has created a condition where radical groups have formed informal bonds and attracted more members by gaining popular sympathy.

As part of the government's unification plan to confront the insurgency issue, the Ramos administration began talks with insurgents. Some insurgent groups entered peace negotiations with their government while the more radical groups refused. They instead turned to acts of violence and terrorism.

Although the Philippine government continues to face threats from militant Islamic terrorist groups as the ASG and JI, they have recently suppressed the growth of these groups, with the assistance of the U.S. government. "Efforts to track down and destroy the ASG and JI have met with some success, especially in Basilan and Jolo, where U.S. troops advised, assisted and trained the Philippine soldiers"[51] in counterinsurgency. The partnership between the two militaries achieved a significant success in 2006 when they launched a mission after having received information from the U.S. funded Rewards for Information Program. "The Armed Forces of the Philippines began a major offensive against the ASG and JI on the island of Jolo. This offensive was remarkably successful and resulted in the deaths of Abu Sayyaf leader Khadafy Janjalani and his deputy, Abu Solaiman".[52]

In many ways, the Philippine government's application of hard power contributed to the growth of insurgencies. But there's a general consensus that the joint efforts of the Armed Forces of the Philippines and the U.S. military has reduced the radical groups in number and capability.

G.   PHILIPPINE SOFT POWER AND NOÖPOLITIK

According to the State Department's country book, "The great majority of the Philippine population is bound together by common values and a common religion."[53] The country book further breaks down the 88.71 million people in the Philippines as 94% Christian (85% Catholic, 9% Protestant), 5% Muslim, and 1%

---

[51] Allen G. Miller, "Philippines: Counterinsurgency Campaign", Edited by Ronald E. Dolan (1991) http://www.libraryofcongress.gov (Accessed on January 28, 2008).

[52] "Rewards for Justice Pays $10 Million in Philippines; $5 Million Reward Each Paid for Two Abus Sayyaf Terrorist Leaders" (June 7, 2007).
http://www.rewardsforjustice.net/index/cfm?page=p_payout&language=english; (Accessed on March 10, 2008).

[53] Chester L. Hunt, "Philippines Religious Life," Edited by Ronald E. Dolan (1991) http://www.libraryofcongress.gov (Accessed on January 28, 2008).

Buddhist or other.[54] The Christian majority makeup of the Philippine society and, likewise, the Philippine government has divided the Filipinos along religious lines. Throughout Philippine history, the Christians have enjoyed political control and economic advantages over the Muslims. Furthermore, years of government neglect have fueled the resentment for the Moro insurgency.

The unstable relationship between the Christians and Muslims contributed to the volatile political conditions that still exist today. The longstanding tension largely stems from the disproportionate wealth of the Christian upper class and the poorest of the poor Muslims. The wealth of the religious elites was often acquired by illegal means in a corrupt system. The Moros assert that they are marginalized by the government, and they are "distrustful of any peaceful efforts as possible ploys to further expand the government's control over the people, the land and its resources. Ongoing land disputes are among the major factors preventing reconciliation between Christians and Muslims."[55] The predominately Christian government continues to face resistance from the minority Muslim population in Mindanao to integrate them into the national mix. The government simply lacks legitimacy in the eyes of the Moros which further alienates the people from their government.

However, "a significant breakthrough occurred with the 1990 establishment of an autonomous region in Mindanao where the majority of the Muslim population is concentrated. The establishment of the Autonomous Region of Muslim Mindanao (ARMM) gave Muslims in this region control over some aspects of government, but not over national security or foreign affairs."[56] Unfortunately, the limitations placed on the local government in the ARMM is viewed by some Muslims as short of their desired full autonomy, and they feel betrayed by the negotiations. In fact, this sense of betrayal has created break-

---

[54] Chester L. Hunt, "Philippines Religious Life," Edited by Ronald E. Dolan (1991) http://www.libraryofcongress.gov (Accessed on January 28, 2008).

[55] Ross Marlay, "Philippines Regional Autonomy," Edited by Ronald E. Dolan (1991) http://www.libraryofcongress.gov (Accessed on January 28, 2008).

[56] Chester L. Hunt, "Philippines: Muslim Filipinos" Edited by Ronald E. Dolan (1991) http://www.libraryofcongress.gov (Accessed on January 28, 2008).

away groups such as the MILF and ASG that have rejected the peace accords and its terms. Despite the Philippine government's efforts to appeal to the Moros through diplomatic engagements and peace talks, Manila's soft power approach is simply lacking. This is not surprising given the tense history of the parties concerned.

H.   A NOÖSTRATEGY TO BALANCE SOFT AND HARD POWER

As the Philippine government's soft power has decreased, the militant Islamic groups' ability to influence and co-opt the Moros has subsequently increased. The U.S. recognizes that, in order to deal with the immediate terrorist threat and meet broader Philippine national issues, it must provide economic aid, military training, and civil-military programs to build a mutually supportive relationship between the Philippine government and its people. Much success has been attributed to the civil-military programs that aim to limit the influence of the militant Islamic groups and the local people, especially in regions where the ASG is known to operate. However, critics warn that U.S. involvement could at best weaken the fragile peace negations between the Philippine government and the MILF, and, at worst, motivate potential groups to join the militants.

Still, President Arroyo faced an increasingly hostile situation in Mindanao with a growing violent Islamic insurgency, while the Philippine military's capability to deal with this issue declined. In response to the situation, President Arroyo "requested U.S. help in suppressing the continually escalating insurgent threat in the south and agreed to allow U.S. forces to train Philippine troops to be more effective in the new Global War on Terrorism."[57]   This partnership was the beginning of a joint exercise, Balikatan, that would improve the Armed Forces of the Philippines' ability to confront the terrorist groups in the southern Philippines while protecting Philippine sovereignty. The joint exercise included classic counterinsurgency training that increased the trust between the people and the Armed Forces and improved the legitimacy of the Philippine government by

---

[57] Cherilyn Walley, "A Century of Turmoil: America's Relationship with the Philippines" *Special Warfare;* September 2004, p. 10.

meeting the needs of the Philippine people on Basilan. In order to assess the needs of the people, they conducted a humanitarian survey of "60,000 of the island's 350,000 residents that dealt with socio-economic trends and living conditions."[58] This led to humanitarian assistance projects such as digging wells, improving roads, and building schools, medical and dental clinics.

Due to the hostile environment on Basilan, and a recognition of the province as the ASG's stronghold, non-governmental organizations had not been to Basilan since the late 1990s. In fact, "the insurgents had driven away all schoolteachers and medical personnel outside the predominantly Christian villages of Lamitan and Isabela, leaving the majority-Muslim islanders without adequate health care or educational opportunities. The water was not safe to drink, and there was little or no electricity."[59] Through the humanitarian projects, however, the AFP on Basilan built a rapport with the people that helped establish a positive relationship between the Basilan people and their national government. Although the effects of soft power and noopolitik are powerfully effective as seen on Basilan, they are often employed in subtle ways, to include public statements of support and partnership.

During a Commemoration for Victims and Heroes of Terrorism, on July 20, 2007, the U.S. Ambassador to the Philippines, Kristie A. Kenney, made the following comments:

> We especially remember the Filipino victims of the 2005 "Valentine's Day" bombings, 2004 SuperFerry bombing, the 2000 Rizal Day bombing, and far too many more. We can defeat terrorism by joining together as one international community composed of different nations, faiths, and cultures to reject the fear and violence of terrorism; remember and respect its victims; and rededicate ourselves to offering communities in conflict-affected areas hope through development, education, and jobs.

---

[58] Cherilyn Walley, "Civil Affairs: A Weapon of Peace on Basilan Island" *Special Warfare;* September 2004, p. 30.

[59] Cherilyn Walley, "Civil Affairs: A Weapon of Peace on Basilan Island" *Special Warfare;* September 2004, p. 31.

America is proud to stand with you, Madame President; the Filipino people; and representatives of the international community as we reject terrorism and violence, and as we respect and honor the heroes of peace and freedom, and the victims of acts of terrorism. And also as we work together to rebuild so that people have hope, so that communities have education and jobs and a future to look forward to, so that we create a brighter world where the future is not only peaceful but also prosperous.[60]

By publicly announcing the U.S.'s support for the Philippine government's efforts in their mutual effort to fight terrorism, the U.S. Ambassador was not only bolstering confidence in the Philippine government, but also promoting stability by assuring their citizens that this is a shared goal. The U.S. Ambassador's message of support to the Philippine government shaped the political, security and information environments in an indirect manner that potentially will have long term effects.

I. MILITANT MOROS HARD POWER

Despite the Moro's desire for autonomy, they have not historically agreed to what this means or how to achieve it. Part of the problem stems from the fact that the Moros are ethnically divided by language and the practice of Islam. According to Graham Turbiville, "the Tausugs, the first group to adopt Islam criticized the more recently Islamicized yakan and bajau peoples for being less zealous in observing Islamic tenets and practices."[61] These internal differences among Moros have added to the instability in Mindanao. While the Moros desire to create an independent Muslim nation, they do not agree on how to pursue independence.

The disagreement within the Moro community has created more radicalized Muslim groups. The MNLF and its military arm, the Bangsa Moro

---

[60] Kristie A. Kenney, U.S. Ambassador to the Philippines, July 21, 2007, "Remarks Commemoration for Victims and Heroes of Terrorism Malacanang Palace", http://manila.usembassy.gov/wwwhs236.html, (Accessed on February 17, 2008).

[61] Graham H. Turbiville, Jr., "Bearers of the Sword: Radical Islam, Philippines Insurgency, and Regional Stability", *Military Review* (Mar-Apr 2002), http://www.smallwars.quantico.usmc.mil/search/lessonslearned/philippines/bearers.asp#end57. (Accessed on January 21, 2008).

Army of an estimated 30,000 men, gained the support of Muslim backers in Libya and Malaysia.[62] Differing goals and tribal rivalries led to a leadership split that created a breakaway group, the MILF. Although smaller and more conservative than the original group, the MILF was well armed and continued to engage in conflict with the government. To further complicate the issue, a more radical Muslim insurgent group, the ASG, entered the scene in the early 1990s. Although the region has experienced periods of ceasefire, these have not led to sustained peace. Government attempts at national reconciliation through diplomatic discussions and the establishment of an autonomous but not independent Muslim area pacified the Moros for a brief period; however, there is no sign that the Moro movement is over.

J.   MILITANT MORO SOFT POWER AND NOÖPOLITIK

Many experts believe that the root cause of terrorism is not poverty or lack of literacy or even lack of employment but rather ideology, a set of beliefs or ideas. Extremist interpretations of Islam and the belief that Moros are being discriminated against and are marginalized are appealing to those who have been neglected by their government. To compound the issue, these Muslims lack legitimate means to make changes in their society. This compels otherwise non-violent Muslims to actively or passively support terrorism. This certainly is not a condition unique to Islam. In fact, throughout history, all major religions have attracted followers and compelled them to employ violence. It seems that moderates of every religion are still struggling with an effective way to dampen this appeal.

What makes this issue even more challenging is the Moros' effective practice of using websites to reach a broad audience. Specifically, the Moros have created a network capable of reaching audiences worldwide through the internet on websites as www.luwaran.com, www.moroland.net (not active),

---

[62] Graham H. Turbiville, Jr., "Bearers of the Sword: Radical Islam, Philippines Insurgency, and Regional Stability", *Military Review* (Mar-Apr 2002), http://www.smallwars.quantico.usmc.mil/search/lessonslearned/philippines/bearers.asp#end57. (Accessed on January 21, 2008).

www.bangsamoro.com, www.bangsamoro.info, and www.mindanews.com. The content on these websites ranges from general information about Islam to sensationalized articles that discredit the government to more edgy videos displaying attacks against the Moros, all with the intention of advancing the Moros' own political agenda.. The websites also carry academic papers and editorials to appeal to a more sophisticated audience. In addition to using websites, MILF sympathizers are increasingly using YouTube to post videos to reach a booming global audience of YouTube visitors.

The power of these multimedia websites, although difficult to fully measure, should not be overlooked. Most of these websites have discussion forums, online chat rooms, and blogs where people can voice their opinions as well as make contact with others. The Moros have created a web resource to expand their cause by using information, whether accurate or not, to reach a growing population of internet users and to attract more followers. Although the general public in Mindanao still lacks internet access, and the Philippines lag behind other Asian countries in internet users, the market is growing and new technology is making the internet more readily accessible through other means such as cell phones, due to both the government's initiatives to expand development and a growing tech savvy population. In a poll conducted in 2007 by Internet World Stats, there are 14 million internet users in the Philippines.[63] Although still relatively low compared to other Asian countries, the Philippines internet market is quickly growing. Between 2005 and 2006, the number of users doubled.[64] The majority of these users are between the ages of 13 to 30 years old, which is also the same age group most likely to be recruited into extremist groups who may find the rhetoric on these radical websites appealing.

It is difficult to control information and often counterproductive to counter misinformation. Employing noöpolitik in an indirect manner may be the most effective way to address the Moros' rhetoric. Although not directly addressing

---

[63] Internet World Stats, www.internetworldstats.com/stats3.htm (Accessed September 24, 2008.

[64] Ibid.

any particular issue expressed on the MILF websites, Ambassador Kenny counters their claims that the Philippine government committed genocide against the Moros in order to expand the Christian control over the land. The ambassador's speech to the Pacific Area Special Operations Conference, on April 17, 2007, stated:

> My story starts with two islands. The first is Basilan, an island in the southern Philippines that in 2001 was a place of lawlessness, a place known for kidnap for ransom groups that had kidnapped and later killed Americans and other foreign tourists. Jump forward to November 2006, when I visited Basilan – not to participate in a kidnap for ransom scheme, but to have lunch at Jollibee, a fast food restaurant, with several of my diplomatic colleagues. We were there talking about peace and development, but interestingly what the people of Basilan wanted to talk about was investment and tourism. The tide has clearly changed.
>
> My story next takes us to an island even further south, the island of Jolo. When I arrived in the Philippines a year ago, I went to Jolo and found in Jolo City people who were wary, bordering on hostile. There was not a lot of activity on the streets and people were edgy about their own military and certainly not particularly interested in seeing U.S. military and U.S. officials in their city. I visited Jolo again a few months ago, in March 2007, and this is the scene I saw: People who were eager to talk to us; street vendors who wanted to say hello; people greeting their own military as if they were heroes; people eager to see Americans; and people who were optimistic about their future even if challenges still remain.
>
> These are just two of the many islands that are winning the war on terrorism in the Philippines.[65]

K.   CONCLUSION

Clearly, the current image of the U.S. and its decline in soft power and noöpolitik warrant a closer examination. The crux of the counter-insurgency problem centers on how much hard versus NoöPower is needed and under what circumstances. Using power effectively involves more than employing precision

---

[65] Kristie A. Kenney, U.S. Ambassador to the Philippines, April 21, 2007, "Speech to the Pacific Area Special Operations Conference," http://manila.usembassy.gov/wwwhs236.html, (Accessed on February 17, 2008).

bombing or applying economic sanctions. The art of influencing behavior through either attraction or co-optation can wield more power than coercion or inducement alone. As Nye states, "Power has never solely flowed from the barrel of a gun; even the most brutal dictators relied on attraction as well as fear."[66]

The United States and other advanced democracies will win the war against terrorists only if the people of any country support their government over radical groups. The ability to attract the population is critical to victory. The U.S. needs to adopt policies that appeal to the foreign and domestic masses, to use public diplomacy more effectively to explain common interests with the public, to stop squandering its soft power, and to learn better how to combine the elements of NoöPower with hard power if it is to meet current challenges.[67]

As noted earlier, a well-run military can be a source of soft power. The impressive job of the U.S. military in providing disaster relief following the 2004 typhoons in Quezon region, or humanitarian assistance during the 2005 Indian Ocean tsunami, or medical aid and recovery operations for the mudslide victims on the island of Leyte helped restore the attractiveness of the United States. In addition, military-to-military cooperation and training programs, for example, can establish transnational networks that enhance a country's soft power.[68] This is especially important in an environment where there are groups as the MILF exerting soft power by propagating their agenda through misinformation. Soft power is an essential element in achieving national interests and deterring terrorist activities. Those who do not fully understand or accept this reality will suffer the consequence of losing power to those who do.

---

[66] Nye, "The Benefits of Soft Power." 47.

[67] Nye, "Soft Power and Leadership," http://www.hks.harvard.edu/leadership/Pdf/SoftPowerandLeadership.pdf (Accessed on January 29, 2008).

[68] Joseph Nye, *Think Again: Soft Power*, February 2008, Bedlam Beat, http://bedlambeat.blogspot.com/2008/02/think-again-soft-power.html, (Accessed on 27 April 2008).

THIS PAGE INTENTIONALLY LEFT BLANK

III.   MINDANAO/BASILAN HISTORY

A.   INTRODUCTION OF ISLAM

The Philippine Islands were largely undisturbed by regional influences until trade began with India, China, and Japan in the 9th century. Before the exogenous influences of Europe, the Middle East, and other Asian countries were introduced, most Filipinos (aside from the established rice farmers on Luzon) had no concept of territoriality, and identity was essentially associated with the *barangay* – the equivalent to a small village.[69] Any group identity extending outside the barangay likely did not exist until the arrival of Islam during the Middle Ages.

Islam arrived in and spread throughout the southern Philippines by two primary means: Islamic merchants and missionaries. The conversion of many of the inhabitants of Mindanao, Basilan, and the Sulu Archipelago left an indelible impression on the indigenous population.

Muslim traders frequently passed through the southern Philippines, many of them settling along the Malayo-Indonesian archipelago. There were several reasons for this, but one factor essentially forced traders to settle – at least temporarily – and that was the weather. The trade winds blow in semi-annual intervals. For six months, the winds primarily blow from west to east. These winds carried the merchants to Asia. The winds then change direction for approximately the same length of time. In the days of sail, merchants had few options during this time other than waiting for the winds to change so that they could return home. Subsequently, many of the traders (mostly men) settled along the routes.

Trade between Islamic merchants and Filipinos began as early as the Ninth Century. As trade expanded throughout Southeast Asia along the Malay-Indonesia and Sulu archipelagos, so did the proliferation of Islam in the southern

---

[69] Ronald E. Dolan, ed. "*Philippines: A Country Study*", (Washington: GPO for the Library of Congress, 1991).

Philippines. Because of their proximity to the trans-Asian trade routes, many southern Philippine islands were populated by transient merchants.[70] These transients gradually became permanent residents of the islands and the local villages. Often the islanders welcomed the merchants, primarily because of the wealth and trading power the merchants brought with them. Traders were often wealthier than the indigenous people, which made them influential within the local communities.

By the 13th century, Islam was established in the Sulu Archipelago, and the once transient Muslims were fully integrated into the micro-societies of the Sulu Archipelago islands. Islam continued to flourish along the trans-Asian trade routes and along the Sulu Archipelago to Mindanao.[71] Among the many missionaries who spread Islam in the southern Philippine islands, there were two who stood above the others.

By many accounts, Karim ul' Makhdum was the first Islamic missionary to reach the Sulu Archipelago, arriving in 1380. Subsequent visits by Arab Muslim missionaries bolstered the spread of Islam in the southern islands; however, by the mid-Sixteenth Century, Muslims had settled as far north as Manila. Makdum's legacy was likely an inspiration for another influential Muslim leader who would follow him more than a century later.

Sharif Kabungsuwan, a foreign prince, was another prominent leader in the expansion of Islam to the Philippines and, more specifically, to Mindanao. According to Hannbal Bara, professor at Mindanao State University, Kabungsuwan was instrumental in uniting Muslims and establishing the sultanates within the region.

> The full Islamization of the west coast of Mindanao was accelerated
> with the arrival of Muhammad Sharif Kabungsuwan. Like Abubakar,
> the first sultan of Sulu, Sharif Kabungsuwan is also an Arab and a
> descendant of Nabi Muhammad (S.A.W.)....He was accompanied

---

[70] Carmen A. Abubakar, "Islam in the Philippines", http://www.ncca.gov.ph/about_cultarts/comarticles.php?artcl_Id=232.

[71] Bruce B. Lawrence, "The Eastward Journey of Muslim Kingship," *Oxford History of Islam*, John Esposito ed. (New York: Oxford University Press, 1999), 421-422.

by large group of Sama people who according to Dr. Kurais, a Sama scholar Kabungsuwan had passed by Tawi-Tawi and picked up some Sama people to accompany him in his journey to Mindanao. This means that the coming of Kabungsuwan to Mindanao was not accidental. It was the Sama people who guided him to Mindanao. During this period, inter-island contact was already in place. Both the Sama and the Iranun had already explored the many sea routes in the Sulu archipelago.

It was not long after his arrival that Sharif Kabungsuwan established the Sultanate of Maguindanao, possibly in 1516. The rise of this sultanate is almost similar to that of Sulu, should be viewed as the culmination of Islamization in Mindanao. It was actually a political necessity. Clearly, the sultanate was adopted as an instrument to consolidate the emerging Muslim communities [Grammar and punctuation are as written in the original document].[72]

The sultanates empowered Muslims and established a solidarity among them that was not seriously challenged until the arrival of the Europeans. The cohesion among Muslims facilitated the expansion of Islam, and Islamic missionaries continued to proselytize unabated in the southern Philippines until the arrival of the Spanish in the Sixteenth Century.

B.   SPANISH COLONIALISM (1521-1898)

The Spanish came to the Philippines in the Sixteenth Century, intending to colonize the islands. One of their first orders of business was to convert the entire archipelago to Catholicism as part of a larger campaign to forestall the spread of Islam in Southeast Asia.[73] European powers had little or no interest in wielding soft power and primarily focused on exercising their hard power assets. The Spaniards were no different and were likely motivated by an intense hatred

---

[72] Hannbal Bara, "The History of the Muslims in the Philippines", http://www.ncca.gov.ph/about_cultarts/comarticles.php?artcl_Id=232.

[73] Peter Chalk, "Militant Islam Extremism in the Southern Philippines" in Jason F. Isaacson and Colin Rubinstein (editors), Islam in Asia: Changing Political Realities (New Brunswick and London: Transaction, 2002), 187-222.

of Muslims that resonated from Moorish domination of the Iberian Peninsula from the Eighth to the end of the 15th century.[74]

The colonial government had negligible success against militant Muslims living in the southern Philippines and never really controlled these Muslim areas. Muslim insurgents used vintas, small wind-propelled vessels, to conduct raids on Spanish strongholds. The introduction of steam-powered boats gave the Spanish an advantage, as did the fort they built in Zamboanga, on the southwest tip of Mindanao. The Spaniards used the fort as a platform to launch raids against militant strongholds in the region.[75] This campaign was marginally successful. Raids in Basilan in 1845, in Jolo in 1876, and in the Lake Lanao region, coupled with Spanish political pressure, were enough to marginalize the sultanates, and eventually led to their collapse. Still, Muslims continued to engage and resist the Spanish, and prevented the colonizers from ever truly controlling the southern islands.

Spanish rule ended in 1898 as a result of Spain's defeat in the Spanish-American War. Subsequently, the U.S. assumed control of the Philippines under the terms of the Treaty of Paris. Unfortunately the treaty existed only between the U.S. and Spain; the same fissures still existed between the disenfranchised Moro population and its colonial occupier.

C.   U.S. COLONIALISM (1898-1946)

Moro insurgents continued to resist colonialism during the period of American rule. In fact, from 1901 to 1904, insurgents in Sulu carried out a guerilla campaign against American forces. The insurrection undoubtedly influenced President Theodore Roosevelt's decision to suspend the Bates

---

[74] Peter Chalk, "Militant Islam Extremism in the Southern Philippines" in Jason F. Isaacson and Colin Rubinstein (editors), Islam in Asia: Changing Political Realities (New Brunswick and London: Transaction, 2002), 187-222.

[75] Paul A. Rodell, "The Philippines and the Challenge of Transnational Terrorism", *Terrorism and Violence in Southeast Asia: Transnational Challenges to States and Regional Stability*, Paul J. Smith ed., (New York: M.E. Sharpe, Inc., 2005), 124.

Treaty[76] and mount an aggressive counter-insurgency campaign against the militant Moros. Retaliation by U.S. forces was heavy-handed and had little regard for soft power effects, as was evidenced by the battle of Bud Bagsak, where more than 500 Muslims and only a handful of Americans were killed. To the Moro population, brutish behavior by a colonial power was commonplace and noosphere was dominated by way of the military facet of hard power. The Moros received little sympathy from U.S. elites, as evidenced by Woodrow Wilson's foreign policies in the Philippines.

When Wilson was elected president in 1912, he shifted American policy to "Filipinization," which integrated Filipinos into the national government.[77] Those Filipinos given government positions were generally Christian, leaving the Muslims with little or no representation. Filipinization resulted in a shift from a policy of brutality to one of discrimination. Furthermore, there were likely few Filipino Christians who were interested in or cared about Moro demands and civil rights.[78]

Wilson introduced a relocation policy that further exacerbated the pre-existing tensions between Filipino Christians and Muslims. The relocation policy encouraged Christians to move to Mindanao, which historically had been Moro land. Christian settlers continued to occupy Muslim lands for decades, widening the fissure between two groups. Relocation was so extensive that the Muslim population on the island was reduced from 76 percent in 1903 to just 32 percent in 1948.[79] During its colonial rule, most American policies involving the Moro population, including Filipinization, were counter-productive and did not endear the colonial or Filipino governments to the Muslims. Centuries-old grievances were left unresolved, and the emerging independent Filipino government was ill-equipped to deal with them.

---

[76] Bates Treaty – Peace treaty signed between the U.S. Brigadier General John Bates and the Sultanate of Sulu, Jamalul Kiram II, on August 20, 1899.

[77] Rodell, 125.

[78] Ibid.

[79] Ibid.

D.   PHILIPPINE INDEPENDENCE (1946-PRESENT)

The end of World War II also brought about the end of American colonialism in the Philippines. In 1946, Filipinos were granted their independence for the first time in more than 400 years. Philippine independence coincided with the resurgence of Islam that occurred throughout the Middle East, and both South and Southeast Asia following World War II, opening the door for renewed Muslim calls for independence.

Since independence, the Philippines have been led by a number of corrupt presidents. Several were oppressive, and not only to Muslims. Every president since independence has been a Christian, which further fans the flames of Muslim discord. Taken together, all of these factors acted as a catalyst to galvanize extremists to commit terrorist acts, either directly or indirectly, against the Philippine government.

E.   FORMATION OF EXTREMIST ORGANIZATIONS

The Moros have been oppressed for centuries. On many occasions, they resisted their oppressors, but these campaigns were largely ineffective, as evidenced by their continued subjugation to the central government and the absence of a Muslim state in the southern Philippines. There are likely several factors that hindered Moro independence movements, including a lack of resources, lack of unity, and a growing constituency. Muslim influence in the southern Philippines increased when the Moros themselves began to organize. This began in the late 1960s in the form of the Muslim Independence Movement (MIM).

Datu Udtug Matalam, an ardent advocate for Moro independence, initiated the MIM in 1968 after the AFP and Christian militias in the region engaged in a series of massacres against Muslim villages. There is no evidence to prove that Matalam authorized or sanctioned any armed resistance to the AFP; however, some members who were outraged by the atrocities organized themselves into a new faction.

The MNLF surfaced as an offshoot of the MIM, but with more ambitious goals than the parent organization. The MNLF partnered with the Bangsa Moro Army (BMA), giving the organization the hard power that for centuries many Moros had desired. Hard power brought clout domestically and internationally. Despite an early military defeat in Jolo, the MNLF rebounded and became increasing more successful in its engagements with the AFP.[80]

A few prominent leaders emerged into leadership positions within the Front. Nur Misauri and Hashim Salamat were two of the more influential leaders in the vanguard of the new Islamic movement. Misauri eventually assumed leadership of the MNLF; Salamat and a few other upstarts contributed to the evolution of the MNLF into a formidable, relevant movement.

The Front's campaign against the Philippine central government was successful until the surge of AFP troops into the southern Philippines in 1975. A stalemate between the MNLF and the government of the Philippines ensued, forcing both to negotiate a peace accord that was codified in the 1976 Tripoli Agreement. As a result, Misauri's influence among Moros declined and the MNLF was severely weakened.[81]

Salamat and several other hard-line Islamists were dissatisfied with the peace agreement and the compromises that Misauri made in it. Once again, the Moro resistance split and Salamat created a new faction of the MNLF that adhered to the earlier principles of the organization. (Another Islamic group, the Bangsa Moro Liberation Organization, was also formed but never gained the support of the Organization of the Islamic Conference [OIC] and quickly became irrelevant.)

Salamat intended to create an institution that concentrated on Islam.[82] With the support of Libya and the OIC, he formed the MILF, with a doctrine

---

[80] Rodell, 128.

[81] Ibid. 129.

[82] Cesar Adib Majul, "The Moro Struggle in the Philippines", *Third World Quarterly* 10, no. 2, (1988), 910.

primarily based on religion rather than on the social issues that were the focus of the MNLF. In 1984, Salamat formally commissioned the MILF and immediately resumed a campaign for Muslim independence.

F.   CONCLUSION

Prior to the arrival of Spanish colonizers in 1521, there was no evidence of religious violence in Philippines. The Spanish successfully proselytized many of the indigenous population on the northern and central islands of the Philippines, but ran into stiff resistance when trying to convert Muslims to Catholicism. It is obvious that, at that time, many Filipinos considered themselves part of a larger group, whether that was Muslim or Catholic. A pronounced division soon appeared among Filipinos that has endured for almost five centuries. Oppressive occupation by both the Spanish and the Americans, coupled with an independent Philippine government dominated by Catholics that discriminated against Muslims, was arguably the root of Muslim grievances. As a result, an insurrection ensued that persisted for much of the Spanish and American colonial periods and has continued to this day, even as Filipinos govern themselves.

IV. COMPARATIVE ANALYSIS

A. BACKGROUND

The Republic of the Philippines is the unwilling host to several organizations that are designated as terrorist groups by the United Nations. According to the Terrorism Knowledge Base website, more than fifteen terrorist organizations have recently conducted or continue to conduct illicit activity within its borders[83]. This chapter will focus on the active, major Islamic extremist organizations that are indigenous to the Philippines.

Shortly after Philippine independence in 1946, the Moros became increasingly aware of their Muslim identity. Moro dissatisfaction with the Philippine government increased during this period, as Muslims were marginalized by political and economic exclusion by the Philippine central government. At the same time, many Moros left the south to study in Manila and the Middle East. These students established personal relationships with Muslims from other countries and regions, developing deep bonds that, in some cases, would be renewed in subsequent years. Through these social networks, dissident Moros organized politically and demanded that the government in Manila establish an independent Moro state.

B. MNLF

The first relevant organization formed was the MNLF, founded by Nurallaji Misuari, who was an alumnus of and former lecturer at the University of the Philippines. While at the university, Misuari was a student activist; he was also one of the organizers of the Mindanao Independence Movement, the forerunner of the MNLF.

The MNLF matured into a viable political organization with a concomitant military branch that rivaled the AFP. During the early to mid 1970s, the MNLF

---

[83] Terrorism Knowledge Base, http://www.tkb.org/GroupRegionModule.jsp?countryid=RP&pagemode=group&regionid=5, (Accessed on February 2, 2008).

and the AFP clashed in several lethal engagements. As a result, the Philippine government signed a treaty that granted the Moros an autonomous region, the Autonomous Region of Muslim Mindanao, or ARMM. The treaty was successful at ending hostilities within the region but only temporarily. Many Moros were displeased with the treaty because it fell short of achieving a separate state for the Muslim population. Shortly after the treaty, the MNLF's power and influence withered and its constituents waned as many Moros still wanted more than autonomy; they wanted their own state. A splinter group quickly took root and addressed Muslim issues

C.   MILF

Extremist organizations are prone to fragmentation, and the MNLF was no exception. Salamat Hashim, a former contender for MNLF leadership, was dissatisfied with the autonomy agreement and Misuari's increasingly moderate ideology shift.[84] Hashim had been a student at Al-Azhar University in Egypt and, like Misuari, had networked with many fundamentalists and extremists while studying there. In 1969, having completed all but the dissertation phase of his doctoral program, Hashim rose to prominence in the Moro community due to his ambition and charisma. [85] He later became one of the most prominent figures in the MNLF prior to breaking off and forming his own group, the Moro Islamic Liberation Front. The MILF was not immune to fractionalization. Many hard-line Islamists were dissatisfied with the faction's compromises and concessions to the GRP. Khadaffy Janjalani organized a small group of extremists that continued the separatist movement under the banner of the Abu Sayyaf Group.

---

[84] "Southern Philippines Backgrounder: Terrorism and the Peace Process", *International Crisis Group,* http://www.crisisgroup.org/home/index.cfm?id=2863&l=1, 3, (Accessed on February 2, 2008).

[85] Ibid.

D. ASG

Janjalani and his corps of separatists had an inauspicious beginning, in spite of their intention to become a relevant organization. Early ASG operations primarily consisted of criminal activities like robbery and kidnapping for ransom; however, the group reinvented itself and significantly increased its constituency, support, and legitimacy. In recent years the ASG has become a viable opponent to the GRP and AFP. As the chart in Figure 1 illustrates, the ASG is the most active and lethal terrorist group currently operating in the Philippines. Prior to 9/11, the ASG controlled significant sections of Mindanao, Tawi Tawi, and Jolo. They essentially supplanted the GRP on Basilan island as the governing body there. As previously mentioned, the ASG and its ties to the JI make it the most significant terrorist threat to security in the Philippines.

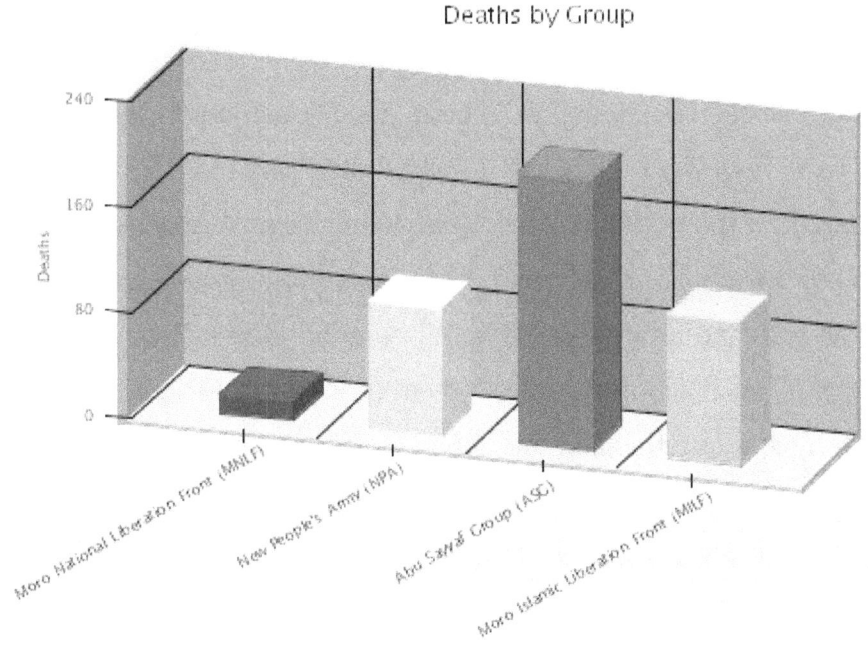

Figure 3. Deaths by Group

Studying the conditions that contributed to the emergence of Islamic extremism is necessary to understand contemporary extremist factions. Islamic extremism in the Philippines originated on the island of Mindanao and several smaller satellite islands off its coast, including the Sulu Archipelago. As explained in the previous chapters, Spanish, U.S., and GRP policies contributed to the dissatisfaction of many Moros living in the southern islands. This dissatisfaction increasingly found expression in the form of terrorism. At the commencement of the GWOT, the island of Basilan was the site where the ASG was most active.

E.   PRE 9/11

The majority of Filipinos embraced their independence from the U.S., but social cleavages existed between Muslims and Christians. It could be argued that, in fact, the cleavage grew in the last half century. There were a variety of reasons for this, most notably Christian dominance within the GRP (as mentioned in the previous chapter).

Prior to 9/11, political, social, and economic conditions on Mindanao, Basilan, Jolo and Tawi Tawi were abysmal. Lawlessness was the norm. Law-abiding citizens feared for their personal safety while miscreants operated freely outside the law. The AFP could not achieve a hard or soft power advantage over the insurgents. It was routine for the AFP to use heavy-handed tactics in dealing with the Moro people. The Philippine central government and AFP leaders erred by adopting a strategy that emphasized the use of violent military force towards the Moro population, rather than a strategy that addressed Moro grievances. Given the belligerent policy towards Muslims, it's of little surprise that extremism proliferated in the southern Philippines prior to 9/11.

F.   POST 9/11

In the wake of al Qaeda's 9/11 attacks against the U.S., President Bush initiated the Global War on Terrorism (GWOT). He and his administration began by reaching out to traditional allies. One of the first leaders he contacted was President Arroyo of the Philippines.

Subsequently, the U.S. dispatched military advisors to the Philippines to assess and assist the AFP and their campaign against the ASG. Shortly after 9/11 and continuing through the end of 2002, the AFP had received more than $93 million in military aid from the U.S., along with a commitment to increase combined training and operations with the U.S. military. AFP commanders welcomed U.S. assistance, and many expressed their desire to have the U.S. military play a significant role in COIN operations on the southern Philippine islands. The Bush administration envisaged a robust force that placed U.S. troops in a direct-action role alongside AFP members; however, the Philippine constitution prohibited foreign militaries from conducting combat operations on Philippine territory. Eventually, the two governments reached an agreement that allowed U.S. forces to conduct operations with their Filipino counterparts by acting mainly as advisors and trainers. However, U.S. and GRP visions of combined operations remained.

U.S. and AFP forces embarked on their new mission in early 2002 in what the GRP advertised as a combined exercise designated Balikatan 02-01,[86] and which the U.S. designated as Operation Enduring Freedom – Philippines, or OEF-P. Because of the political sensitivity involved, the operation names remain unchanged to this day. For the purpose of this paper, it will be referred to as OEF-P.

The first operational forces to deploy in support of OEF-P were part of JTF-510 under the command of Brigadier General Donny Wurster, a U.S. Air Force Officer who then commanded the U.S. Special Operations Command Pacific, or SOCPAC. Wurster's strategy to assist the AFP in counter-insurgency, or COIN, operations was based on a model developed by Gordon McCormick,[87] a professor and department head for the Defense Analysis Department at the Naval Postgraduate School.

---

[86] Balikatan is a Tagalog word that means "shoulder to shoulder."

[87] Gordon McCormick's diamond model for counterinsurgency.

JTF-510's main effort during OEF-P was conducted primarily by Army Special Operations Forces, or ARSOF. ARSOF is composed of Special Forces, Civil Affairs, and Psychological Operations soldiers whose forte is low-intensity conflict. Wurster's senior ARSOF commander during OEF-P was 1st Special Forces Group commander Colonel David Fridovich. A highly-regarded group commander, Fridovich brought extensive knowledge and experience to the Philippines. Army Civil Affairs and PSYOP teams from the U.S. Army Civil Affairs and Psychological Operations Command, or USACAPOC, were placed under his operational control.

One of ARSOF's informal mantras is that execution occurs "by, with, and through the indigenous population." SOCPAC's operations on Basilan were conducted precisely in this way. There were many elements that contributed to the command's success, but it was basic SOF tenets that assured success on the island and the JTF's commitment to low intensity conflict that revealed the potential of applying precision hard and soft power. This can be explained more clearly by comparing the JTF's strategy to Kalev Sepp's COIN best practices, a comparison which strongly suggests that there is a correlation between them. Sepp posits that these twelve critical steps that can focus on the use of hard and soft power must be addressed in order to suppress an insurgency:[88]

1. Emphasis on intelligence;
2. Focus on population, their needs, and security;
3. Secure areas established, expanded;
4. Insurgents isolated from population (population control);
5. Single authority (charismatic/dynamic leader);
6. Effective, pervasive psychological operations (PSYOP) campaigns;
7. Amnesty and rehabilitation for insurgents;
8. Police in lead; military supporting;
9. Police force expanded, diversified;
10. Conventional military forces reoriented for counter-insurgency;

---

[88] Kalev Sepp, "Best Practices in Counterinsurgency", *Military Review*, (May-June 2005) 10.

11.   Special Forces, advisers embedded with indigenous forces;

12.   Insurgent sanctuaries denied.

Each of Sepp's critical COIN tasks was performed by the JTF to varying degrees. The tasks were often mutually supporting. For example, by focusing on the population's needs and security, SOF operators and their AFP partners were able to gather actionable intelligence about the ASG. One could even argue that accomplishing one or more of Sepp's practices would cause a "domino" effect that would assist in completing the other tasks. Securing the populace frequently denies the insurgents sanctuary, which, in turn, isolates them from the populace, which facilitates the expansion of secured areas, and so forth. Sepp's theory is pragmatic and achievable. However, one critical variable that will ultimately determine the success or failure of a COIN operation is a sincere political and military commitment from the host nation's government and the supporting coalition. Without such a commitment, the legitimate government faces the prospect of a protracted fight.

The Bush administration remains committed to assisting the Philippine government in eradicating terrorism. SOCPAC has built on the successes of the Balikatan operations by branching out to other high-risk areas in the Philippines. U.S. – Philippine strategy mirrors Andrew Krepenevich's "Oil Spot" strategy[89]: that is, control of one geographic area is secured and maintained, then operations are expanded to an adjacent area, and this cycle is repeated until the objective is achieved. This was evidenced by recent combined joint task force operations on the islands of Jolo and Tawi Tawi, as well as an expanded effort on Mindanao. Current operations showed an increased emphasis in American soft power aimed at complementing hard power.

---

[89] Andrew Krepinevich, "How to Win in Iraq", *Foreign Affairs*, http://www.foreignaffairs.org/20050901faessay84508/andrew-f-krepinevich-jr/how-to-win-in-iraq.html. (Accessed on February 2, 2008).

G.   CONCLUSION

JTF 510 and JSOTF-P operations on Basilan Island were widely considered by the SOF community to be the model for conducting COIN. A campaign focused on the population and relied more on non-lethal constructive effects rather than the destructive effects of lethal targeting and conventional military force. This focus on noopolitik severely hindered ASG recruiting and resource acquisition. Additionally, the coalition was able to dominate the noosphere while simultaneously wielding non-kinetic hard power in the form of humanitarian assistance. The disaffected Moro population on Basilan finally had its basic needs met by the GRP, resulting in an increase of coalition soft power, and, conversely, a decimating of the ASG's soft power on the island.

The GRP's shift from neglecting Moro needs to concentrating on and addressing them has narrowed the cleavage between the GRP and the Moro population. It is premature to say that the chasm has been completely bridged; however, the evidence suggests that GRP and its coalition partners have made progress by using an approach that combines noopolitik and realpolitik. If the GRP wants sustainable results, it must adopt a long-term strategy that is sustainable and remains focused on the disaffected population.

V. FILIPINO DOMESTIC PERSPECTIVE

To deter and overcome insurgency, government [sic] response must be comprehensive and a multi-disciplinary approach. Legislation should package polices, [sic] plans and programs that directly confront the insurgent threat and simultaneously address its root causes. To achieve this, the government has to adopt a strategy, which is a holistic approach to overcome insurgency nationwide. This consists of four major components: Political / Legal / Diplomatic, socio-economic / psychosocial influences, and peace, order and security. We must include an information campaign that [sic] easily understood by all no matter of literary education.[90]

To adequately understand any problem, it is necessary to study the situation from multiples perspectives. The insurrection in the Philippines is no different. Analyzing from a Filipino perspective the conditions, motives, and opportunities that led to the insurgency will likely provide a better understanding of the problem and, subsequently, result in the best the best course of action for government of the Philippines to bridge the soft power gap.

A. CONDITIONS

Historically political opportunities for Muslims within the central government of the Philippines were virtually non-existent. The Moros faced numerous challenges and obstacles in their efforts to advance their interests domestically and internationally. They have been routinely discriminated against and exploited by the GRP. Because of the exclusive nature of Philippine politics, many Moros lacked an understanding of the established political process. Furthermore, Moro grievances were routinely viewed by Filipino political elites as illegitimate or irrelevant, further inciting Moro disaffection for the government in Manila. In a 2007 interview, Ed Tiongson. Vice President of the

---

[90] Cecilia Dionco, Noble Director of Office of STRATCOM February 8, 2004 1st Barangay Counterterrorism Council Meeting.

Liga ng Barangay,[91] opined on the deficiencies in Moro political opportunities. According to Tiongson, there were five obstacles to Moro political participation[92]:

1. Widespread misperceptions of and acrimony towards Christians.

2. Perceptions that the Christian political majority and elites are not truly committed to the well being of the Moros. Moros also believe that politicians are power-hungry opportunists that have the tendency to extend favors only exclusively to their own clans and political comrades, while showing disregard for their constituents.

3. Moros political agendas largely ignore local politics and neglect their own communities.

4. Incidents of Moro political leaders deceiving, manipulating, and exploiting the high illiteracy rate of the Moro population.

5. A history of neglect by the GRP of the Moro population and their grievances.

To assist in the analysis of these obstacles, as well as the existing social, economic, political, and cultural conditions that moved some Moros to extremism, this thesis incorporated the Political Process Model from the social movement theory. In Figure 1, American author and professor of Sociology Doug McAdam laid the theoretical groundwork for the Political Process Model through the paradigm of opportunities available via the established political structure, and, more specifically, the opportunity for social movement groups to successfully address their grievances.

---

[91] A Barangay is a Filipino community the size of a small town or village. The Liga ng mga Barangay sa Pilpinas is a Philippine government agency that represents approximately 49,000 Barangays.

[92] Personal interview with Mr. Tiongson (2007).

Figure 4.   McAdam's Political Process Model[93]

According to the "Political Opportunity" element of the model, any event or broad social process that serves to undermine the calculations and assumptions on which the political establishment is structured creates a void in political opportunities.[94] The political environment in the Philippines is difficult to penetrate by a Moro population that has created a fissure between the two

As a result, the Moros have gravitated towards the indigenous organizational strength element of McAdam's model. Through the formation of such influential groups like the MNLF, MILF, and ASG; the Moro population has established a "community" that shares cultural understanding, identity, and similar grievances with the GRP. The aforementioned groups have provided a vehicle for radical Islamists to advance their demands for Moro independence. Additionally, exogenous influences, namely radical Islamic groups from Indonesia and the Middle East, have manipulated the groups' perceptions of injustice, stimulating incitement and provoking rebellion.

---

[93] Doug McAdam, *Political Process and the Development of Black Insurgency, 1930-1970*, (The University of Chicago Press, Chicago, 1999), 51.

[94] Ibid, 48.

B.   MOTIVATIONS

Most historians believe that Filipino Muslims began to effectively organize in resistance of the Filipino government shortly after the Jabidah Massacre of 1968. The massacre, which took place in Mindanao, left an estimated 100,000 dead, 200,000 fled to Malaysia, and nearly a million people homeless. Historically many AFP soldiers were unsympathetic to the Moros and routinely violated the human rights of Muslims. From the Moro perspective, the so-called "Manila Imperialists," as part of a Christian attempt to colonize Moro lands, staged the massacre. The incident is remembered every year in many Moro communities, and remains a continuing source of friction. A more thorough explanation of radical Islam's motivations was discussed in Chapter III. Unfortunately, the motives for Islamic Extremism can largely be attributed to the AFP's hard power campaigns against radical and moderate Muslims alike. The AFP's heavy-handed approach widened the Moro-Christian schism and steadily detracted from the government's soft power in the Southern Philippines.

C.   EXTREMIST OPPORTUNITIES

Harsh socio-economic conditions often contribute to extremist motivations, which in turn, inspire terrorists to seek out vulnerable populations that can be leveraged to degrade the state's soft power while bolstering their own. For many years, Moro radicals have sought to exploit weaknesses in the GRP noöpolitik so that the extremists can gain an advantage in the noosphere. Moro radicals have attempted to do this in a variety of ways. In 2006, Moro extremists carried out several violent attacks aimed at degrading GRP soft power by trying to show that the GRP was impotent in the Southern Philippines. During this time, the Philippines endured 93 bombings, ranging from improvised explosive devices and grenades to landmines. Major incidents included:

1.   February - the bombing of a karaoke bar near a Philippine military base in Jolo left one dead and 22 injured;

2.   March - a bomb exploded at the Sulu Consumers Cooperative in Jolo, killing nine people and injuring 20;

3. June - a roadside bombing in Shariff Aguak killed three people and injured eight;

4. August - two bombs exploded almost simultaneously in Kidapawan City, injuring three people;

5. September - a bomb exploded at a public market in General Santos City, killing two people and injuring six;

6. October - a bomb exploded near the headquarters of the Sulu Philippine National Police in Jolo, injuring two people;

7. In a separate October attack, three bombs exploded in Tacurong, Sultan Kudurat; Makilala, North Cotabato; and Cotabato City, killing eight people and injuring over thirty.[95]

It is difficult to determine if the extremists achieved the desired affects from these attacks. At a minimum, the offensive showed how vulnerable the target population was and that the extremists were undeterred by the AFP. It is also likely that these successes invigorated Moro extremists, thus helping them recruit new members and fuel the insurrection.

Vice President Tiongson identified several issues that the government must address if it genuinely wants to quell the insurrection. He posits that citizens are the most important factor in bringing peace, security and development to Mindanao. He also suggests that how children are raised, educated socially, and supported inside the home as well in as the community truly makes a difference. Equally important is the way in which Muslim children and youth are treated and nurtured up to the time they become adolescents. He also recognized the need for Muslim youth to experience loving, secure, and healthy relationships with others in the community. If the people they observe and interact with (parents, friends, neighbors, etc.) provide examples of honest, enlightened and loving relationships, then violence and extremist recruiting would decrease.[96]

---

[95] Country Reports on Terrorism Released by the Office of Coordinator for Counterterrorism April 30, 2007, http://www.state.gov/ct/rls/crt/2006/82731.htm (Accessed 4 July 2008).

[96] Personal interview with Mr. Tiongson (2007).

D.   GRP RESPONSE

The Philippine Government now under President Gloria
Macapagal-Arroyo is faced with myriad problem [sic] in Mindanao
that continues to destabilize the area. The major threats come from
the MNLF-MILF-Abu Sayyaf Group combined and from the
CPP/NPA/NDF program to set up their own concept of government
in Mindanao. The problem, if only internal, may be within the
capacity of the Philippine Government to solve.[97]

Prior to 9/11, the Philippine government was keenly aware that it had a

domestic terror problem and committed extensive resources to combating the

insurgents. Many Filipino political and military elites believed their stagnant

counterterrorism campaign needed a jumpstart that eventually arrived in the

wake of the 9/11 attacks on America.

Almost immediately after 9/11, the Republic of the Philippines redoubled

its bilateral counterterrorism efforts with the United States and to this day

continues its COIN campaign. In August 2005, the Armed Forces of the

Philippines (AFP) launched "Operation Ultimatum," a concerted effort to capture

or kill top Jemaah Islamiya (JI) and Abu Sayyaf Group (ASG) operatives on Jolo

Island. The operation has been highly successful to date, as a number of ASG

and JI members have been either captured or killed since its inception.

The creation of the Antiterrorism Task Force (ATTF) was another aspect

of combined American-Filipino counterterrorism campaign. The ATTF combined

the hard power assets of the Philippine National Police (PNP) and the AFP in

fighting terror. Since its inception, the ATTF has arrested, captured, or killed 88

suspected terrorists, and seized over 900 kilograms of explosive materials.

Additionally, the Task Force has made significant progress in tracking, blocking,

and seizing terrorists' assets.[98]

Perhaps the ATTF's most notable achievement to date occurred between

2006 and 2007 when the AFP eliminated both Khadaffy Janjalani, then leader of

---

[97] Delfin Castro, Major General (Retired), Philippine Army "A Mindanao Story: Troubled
Decades in The Eye of The Storm" Chapter 12: Prognosis.

[98] Country Reports on Terrorism Released by the Office of Coordinator for Counterterrorism
April 30, 2007, http://www.state.gov/ct/rls/crt/2006/82731.htm (Accessed 4 July 2008).

the Abu Sayyaf Group, and former ASG spokesperson Abu Solaiman. Operation Ultimatum demonstrated the emphasis of U.S.-assisted strategy to strengthen the rule of law in the Sulu archipelago. Coupled with the Combined U.S.-Philippine military exercises (Balikatan), the ATTF and the JSOTF-P supported the Philippine government's campaign to separate terrorists from the general population and diminish support for their cause.[99]

In conjunction with the counterterrorism operations, President Gloria Macapagal-Arroyo aggressively established legislation enhancing cooperation between the Republic of the Philippines and U.S. in the War on Terror. *"The Fourteen Pillars of Policy and Action Against Terrorism"*; Memorandum Order No. 37 dated October 12, 2001 included[100]:

1. Supervision and implementation of policies and actions of the Government against terrorism;
2. Intelligence coordination;
3. Internal focus against terrorism;
4. Accountability of public and private corporations and personalities;
5. Synchronizing internal efforts with global outlook;
6. Legal measures;
7. Promotion of Christian and Muslim solidarity;
8. Vigilance against the movement of terrorists and their supporters, equipment, weapons and funds;
9. Contingency plans;
10. Comprehensive security plans for critical infrastructure;
11. Support of overseas Filipino workers;
12. Modernization of the AFP;

---

[99] The Philippine Presidential Commission on the Visiting Forces (VFACOM) is empowered by Executive Order 199 to oversee the implementation of the Visiting Forces Agreement. The VFA Commission is required to annually conduct an assessment and submit a recommendation to the President of the Philippines on whether or not the Agreement continues to serve the national interest.

[100] "RP-US Enhanced Cooperation on the War on Terror", Memorandum Order No. 37, 2001 further specifies the measures that shall be undertaken in connection with the Government's commitment to cooperate in the international struggle against terrorism.

13. Media support;
14. Political, social and economic measures.

President Arroyo's policy addressed the most obvious shortcomings in her government's counter-terrorism policies up to that point and was bolstered by an infusion of support by way of robust economic and military packages from the U.S. and its allies; however, noticeably absent from her policy was a soft-power strategy. Fortunately the GRP adopted a progressive philosophy to combating terrorism and the coalition was able to influence its host to adopt a less "kinetic" approach to COIN operations. With the assistance of the U.S. government and its military forces, the GRP and AFP started to incorporate non-lethal targeting to complement its lethal targeting. Equipped to apply both hard and soft power, the combined Joint Task Force revitalized and enhanced COIN operations in the Philippines.

The Basilan model was designed to use unconventional means by using an indirect approach that employed a combination of both hard and soft power. The first step in this approach was to secure the environment, then to develop infrastructure, and finally, to sustain these efforts. The strategy aimed to not just address terrorism per se, but to eradicate the very roots of terrorism in the Philippines – poor governance. This translates specifically to poverty, the lack of economic opportunities, inaccessibility to economic centers, and the lack of education.

Gaining the support of the people is crucial to the unconventional approach that the U.S. and AFP troops used and are still using in Mindanao. To gain the populace's support, the task force adopted a strategy that emphasized exercising noöpolitik rather than conventional military action. This approach has been well received by many Moros and has won the support of many communities in Mindanao. The effects were almost immediate and could be measured by the decrease in terrorist incidents.

One proof of the success of this strategy is the fact that, in the six years since Balikatan 02-1, there has been a significant reduction of threat groups and crime in Basilan. In 2002, fifteen AFP Battalions were needed to provide security on Basilan. By 2005, after a successful soft power campaign, only two AFP Battalions were deployed in the area to maintain security. This sustained and prevailing peace in Basilan is attributed to the increased socio-economic opportunities, which sharply reduced the local population's support of, and desire to join, terrorist groups.

Basilan now possesses an environment that is conducive to economic activity. From 2002 until today, almost $2.2 million in humanitarian assistance and Civil Military Operations and $4.5 million in USAID initiatives were funneled to the development of Basilan. This translated into 80 kilometers of roads, four bridges and two piers and ramps, five water projects, and a number of medical and dental missions, all of which benefited the island's communities.[101] In fact, because of the strategic success of Basilan and the integration of all three key components and/or military techniques, the model used there has gained acclaim in numerous publications as a means of addressing the international threat of terrorism and eradicating militant Islamic activities in other areas of the globe. Throughout the Philippines, from as far south as the island of Sulu to the northern portion of Central Mindanao, this method has been employed as the blueprint of establishing peace, growth and prosperity.

Strategically and tactically, the Philippine government found a military solution to the immediate threat of terrorist activities within the country, but it has not adequately focused on the political, social and economic aspects of Moro grievances in relation to the Mindanao conflict. The perception of counterinsurgency efforts within the Southern Philippines is one of Filipino Christian self-determination vs. Muslim reformation.

> This is a double edge sword. It may have created dent in the
> insurgents but has widen the wedge of the people and the
> government. The victims are clearly the general populace, and

---

[101] Ms. Michelle Eduarte, a Philippine Government employee in the Department of Foreign Affairs; American Affairs,and a member of the VFA commission, is responsible for providing both quarterly and annual reports and an overseer in relation to RP-US joint counter-terrorism efforts in the Autonomous Region of Muslim Mindanao.

adding "salt" to a suffering, Filipino will only aggravate the situation. Unless effective social mitigation programs are in place, such diverse reactions will always be felt [Grammar and punctuation are as written in the original document].[102]

E.   CONCLUSION

For a little more than six years, the GRP and AFP have successfully campaigned to deter Islamic extremism through multiple indictments of known insurgent members of the ASG, JI, and Al Qaeda. Both domestic and international audiences may assume that U.S. diplomatic pressure forced the GRP to address its terrorist problem; however, the result has been several positive counterterrorism developments: an Anti-Terrorism Bill (or Human Security Act), coordination of Philippine interagency, positive feedback of communities and military to the U.S.'s Rewards for Justice program, elimination of ASG leaders as a result of Operation Ultimatum, and so forth. Other positive U.S. contributions that were well received include such programs as MEDCAPS and USAID-funded life-improvement projects.

Through cooperation between Indonesia, Singapore, the U.S. and Australia, the GRP and AFP realized that conventional tactics alone met with limited success in battling an insurgency. Through a comprehensive approach of combining hard and soft power, they developed several methods of finding and attacking the vulnerabilities in the enemy's "center of gravity." These means have isolated the insurgents from enemy intelligence. They have also affected the insurgents' association with the disenfranchised Muslim communities of the southern Philippines that had provided recruits, training areas, and safe havens. In addition, the government gained support in the rural areas through development programs and social services.

Regrettably, the solutions that have so far been offered by most development partners, government and non-government alike, are only economically focused. These temporary development programs can, at most,

---

[102] Jose Maria Cuerpo III , Major, Philippine Army, In response to an interview on 11 November 2007.

placate or mitigate, but they do not resolve the issues. The real issue is the manner in which Muslim youths are being misled into believing that violence is a viable option.

The seeds of peace must be sown and then nurtured continuously within the Islamic culture, beginning with families, neighborhood groups, and community institutions and so on. The media and the Ligas within the affected areas should also be involved.

Economic approaches are not the only answer to the problems of troubled Muslim youth. Roads, bridges and other infrastructure are helpful, but only when they are paralleled with developing the social infrastructure. The socialization, education, empowerment, and engagement of the youth through meaningful activities designed to enlighten, and enhance growth will deter them from becoming extremist recruits. Thus the pro-active, preventive and people centered Barangay approach is, perhaps, a better approach for both short and long-term peace building strategy.

A holistic, integrated and comprehensive approach is required for the GRP to defeat the insurgents, particularly one that extends beyond the *Fourteen Pillars* and focuses on socio-cultural-political infrastructure in Muslim-populated areas. A strategy that has an end state of egalitarianism throughout the Philippines and that uses all elements of national power is needed. A truly holistic approach is progressive and uses realpolitik and noöpolitik to achieve equilibrium between hard and soft power.

THIS PAGE INTENTIONALLY LEFT BLANK

VI. RECOMMENDATIONS AND CONCLUSION

Seven years after 9/11, the U.S. government is still struggling with how to conduct a war against terrorism. A staggering amount of resources have been exhausted tackling the global threat posed by radical groups. Still, it is questionable how much success the U.S. and its allies have achieved when violent groups are still conducting attacks and recruiting more members each day. In fact, it appears that in places like Iraq and Afghanistan, military action may be contributing to the perception that the U.S. is waging a war against Islam. Sadly, this perception is promoting more violence which justifies the use of violence to combat violence. It's a dangerous cycle.

In the Philippines, the U.S. applied an innovative and simple formula to break the cycle of violence. In fact, it is arguably the most successful campaign launched since 9/11. The joint U.S. and GRP effort focused on the people of southern Philippines and not on directly destroying the insurgents. In fact, focusing on the terrorists may create a stronger bond between the terrorist and their support . Gracia Burhnam, an American missionary who was held hostage by the ASG in Mindanao along with her husband Martin, shares a personal exchange between her and one of her captors, Solaiman who harbored a deep resentment of the west for its "self-indulgence, immorality, and coarseness."[103] Using excessive violence to attack the ASG would have perpetuated this view and compromised efforts to gain the release of the hostages. As previously mentioned in the Basilan case study, disrupting the cycle of violence through a softer approach works. But for how long and to what extent under what circumstances? Does the U.S. need to transform its military so that it is better able to deal with a dynamic environment in a long-term struggle and, if so, in what ways?

---

[103] Gracia Burnham, *In the Presence of My Enemies,* (Wheaton, Illinois: Tyndale House Publishers, Inc, 2003) 104.

A. THE TRANSFORMATION OF WARFARE

More than ten years before the 9/11 attacks, Martin van Creveld, in his book *The Transformation of War,* predicted that conventional war was rapidly becoming obsolete. He explained that, "war will be conducted by groups other than states and by means other than armies."[104] He went on to say that "the control over the modern state is diminishing, the utility of large-scale conventional forces is decreasing, and the nature of war is changing."[105] Of particular interest to this thesis, Van Creveld argues that success in battle will not be guaranteed by high tech weapon systems and a superior military force. That is, technologically sophisticated armies are not effective against unsophisticated forces who have obtained less advanced but more useful means to attack. Van Creveld's prophetic assertion alludes to, perhaps coincidentally, the emergence of soft power and noöpolitik. Today's conflicts straddle between the battlefield and the noosphere. A comprehensive strategy that employs both soft and hard power should be routine when planning conventional and irregular warfare.

America's GWOT has gone divergent paths in the Middle East and Southeast Asia. The situation in Iraq remains tumultuous in spite of the abundance of hard power assets there. Conversely, the AFP and U.S. military are conducting successful COIN operations in the southern Philippines with a fraction of the material. The difference can be attributed to strategy. OIF strategy initially emphasized military power and "shock and awe," whereas, OEF-P strategy emphasized low intensity conflict that employed a combination of both hard and soft power. Fortunately, strategic successes in the Philippines have not gone unnoticed by other combatant commanders. The commander of the Multi-National Force-Iraq, General David Petraeus, has shifted military strategy in Iraq from solely kinetic to a strategy that combines military power, hard power, and soft power.

---

104 Martin Van Creveld, *Transformation of War* (New York: The Free Press, 1991), 109-112.
105 Ibid. 109-112.

B. MILITARY TRANSFORMATION: ORGANIZATIONAL AND IDEOLOGICAL

Some critics question the need to transform the world's best military force or to consider other strategies. However, history and current trends indicate that merely maintaining the present military while attempting to hold on to existing concepts is a shortsighted approach and may prove disastrous. Global enemies in the war on terrorism have transformed, and so must the U.S. military. However, the military must choose its course carefully in order to maximize positive effects. Simply advocating all innovative efforts actually is counterproductive. The U.S. must carefully consider what aspects of transformation will give the best return for the investment. Additionally, a change in military strategy is necessary, one that includes the application of soft power in concert with hard and military powers.

Proponents for transformation suggest that unless the U.S. military adapts to the information age, it may not retain its elite status for long. As the dispersion of information and the rate of technological change continue to accelerate, current U.S. military advantages could diminish comparatively. Furthermore, the former Director of the Office of Force Transformation, Vice Admiral (Ret) Arthur K. Cebrowski states, "We cannot delay transformation while we fight the war on terrorism." [106] If it's largely agreed and widely acknowledged that transformation is necessary, is it possible to fight a war while transforming and, if so, what should be done to move the military in the right direction at the speed required to get ahead? Any change is bound to be disruptive in the short term. However, not changing could be far more troublesome in the long term.

Soft power transformation is not simply a matter of improving current ways of conducting operations, and it is not merely about technology. Former Secretary of Defense Rumsfeld stated, "All the high-tech weapons in the world won't transform our armed forces, unless we also transform the way we think,

---

[106] Paul Stone, "Cebrowski Sketches the Face of Transformation," *U.S. Department of Defense, American Forces Press Service News Articles* (December 29, 2003), http://www.defenselink.mil/news/newsarticle.aspx?id=27559 (Accessed on 23 September 2007).

train, exercise, and fight."[107] In light of the militant Islamic insurgency in Mindanao, it is important to incorporate new soft power strategies into the military to yield optimal benefits.

C.   ISLAMIC EXTREMISM AND THE PHILIPPINES

In recent years, there has been an alarming increase in religiously motivated violence in Southeast Asia. This is not to imply that this violence is a new phenomenon. Rather, history is full of religious conflict which is neither limited to any particular religion nor land. What is it about religion that lends itself to violence? Part of the answer lies in the fact that there is a dark underside of religion that can be dangerous. Even though all the major faiths espouse the values of peace, love, and compassion, sacred scriptures and traditions contain justification for murder and apocalyptic strife. It is the interpretation of the scripture that moves people to act out in anger and revenge in the name of their faith.

Mark Juergensmeyer's concept of "cosmic war" provides a useful framework for examining religiously motivated violence. Cosmic war is broadly characterized by a spiritual confrontation between good and evil and is symbolic, dramatic, and a moral justification for violence where the outcome of the struggle is preordained and victory is imminent. Cosmic war proponents view events in terms of absolutes - right and wrong, good and evil.[108] Juergensmeyer defines cosmic war as the "metaphysical conflicts between good and evil" that "transcend human experience."[109]

When viewing the ASG through western, non-radical, non-religious eyes, we see the ASG as extremely radical. However, they see themselves as soldiers

---

[107] U.S. Secretary of Defense Donald Rumsfeld , "21st Century Transformation of U.S. Armed Forces" (speech given at the National Defense University, Fort McNair, Washington D.C. on January 31, 2002), http://www.defenselink.mil/speeches/speech.aspx?speechid=183 (Accessed on 15 September 2007).

[108] Mark Juergensmeyer, *Terror in the Mind of God,* 3rd ed (Berkeley: University of California Press, 2003), 149.

[109] Ibid. 149.

fighting for the righteous and adhering to the purest form of religion. The spiritual calling to reclaim their faith seems to resonate with the ASG members and sets the stage for hatred which compels its followers to carry out justice. The authority of religion gives the ASG the moral legitimacy to employ violence as a spiritual struggle between good and bad.

Many of its members are attracted to the group's rejection of what they perceive as the largely Christian Philippine government's corruption and neglect of the minority Muslims in Mindanao. The growing tension can also be attributed to the Armed Forces of the Philippines' (AFP) human rights violations. Still, the ASG's brutal beheadings, bombings, and kidnappings are barbaric even if their grievances are understandable.

Rather than focusing on the ASG's extreme world view and use of violence, the U.S. and Philippine governments should look at what they are doing that may cause the tension. Although it may make sense that groups use violence to achieve their goals, it is not preferred. A better understanding of the factors that can contribute to violence and how religion motivates and mobilizes people is essential in developing a soft power strategy to combat this issue. Those who oppose religious terrorism have to find a way of rejecting violence without rejecting the religion.

Furthermore, the Philippines host two religions that have rivaled each other for centuries. In this case the Christian majority has dominated the Muslim minority since the Spanish colonial period. Furthermore, the conditions in the southern Philippines were ripe for an insurgency. Muslim grievances were largely ignored as the situation gradually deteriorated. Consequently, the Moro population became increasing disaffected with their oppressors which ignited an insurrection that has waged intermittently for nearly five centuries. Prior to the reinvigorated cooperation between the U.S. government and the GRP, the AFP had little success in COIN operations and reducing terrorist recruiting.

D. DETERRING EXTREMIST RECRUITING

Is there anything distinctive about Muslims in general and Moros in particular that makes them especially difficult to reform? The ASG is a small group at the extreme end of a hostile subculture in Islam. To most Moros, Janjalani is no more a representative of Islam than Osama Bin Laden is. Still, it is undeniable that the ideals of the MNLF, MILF, and ASG have resonated with thousands of disenfranchised Muslims in the Philippines. Extremists have used religion to justify the use of violence to advance their cause. Janjalani compelled his followers to believe in cosmic war, a spiritual struggle between good and bad. In most cases of religious violence, concepts of cosmic war have been accompanied by claims of moral justification. By studying the factors and identifying the conditions and triggers that galvanize individuals into extremist behavior, a strategy can be developed to retard the process.

Since 9/11, there has been an increasing polarization between Islam and Christianity. Rather than focusing on religious fanatics' extreme world view and use of violence, we should look at what we are doing that may be contributing to the tension. When national leaders claim that the U.S. is at war with evil and will fight to defend America's righteous cause, they are engaging in a cosmic war - and playing into the hands of cosmic warriors. The U.S. government should also consider other factors that motivate and mobilize people to terrorism. Many Muslims cite U.S. foreign policy as their most significant grievance with America.

Too often policy is myopic and developed in a metaphorical vacuum. Joseph Nye defers to Mark Leonard, a British expert on public diplomacy, on this matter. "Leonard warns that many governments make the mistake of explaining domestic decisions only to their domestic audiences and fail to realize the effect of their actions and the explanations of their actions on the international image of their country."[110] A common theme expressed by many foreigners is that they dislike U.S. foreign policies rather than disliking Americans. Joseph Nye referred

---

[110] Nye, 108.

70

to several opinion polls taken in 2002 that measured the attractiveness of America globally. Nearly all regions and demographics surveyed showed a significant larger attractiveness to American technology advances and culture compared to the way America "was doing business."[111] Coincidently the Moros have expressed similar dissatisfaction with the GRP policies. Despite living within the same geographic borders, the GRP has thus far has underachieved in addressing Moros grievances. To win the War on Terror in Philippines, the GRP must institute policies and develop strategies that include the noosphere. Furthermore, the central government in Manila direct all the elements of national power in the form hard and soft power towards the Moro population. If the GRP sincerely commits to resolving the issues discussed throughout this thesis, their prospects for defeating the insurgency are greatly increased.

E.   OPERATIONALIZING SOFT POWER

Over the past decade, the U.S. has largely underachieved in wielding its soft power while focusing primarily developing its hard power throughout the world. For the first time since the Vietnam War, the U.S. is facing a situation in which the appeal of other states and non-state actors is gaining ground and, at times surpassing, U.S. soft power. This change not only affects American influence throughout the world, but is terribly dangerous to national security because it yields precious ground to insurgents. The challenge to operationalizing soft power is understanding what it is and how it can be used as a tool. The key to operationalizing soft power is to identify America's noöpolitik assets and then develop strategies and policies that will boost the nation's soft power.

Joseph Nye addresses America's need for policy change. Nye suggests that, "We need to adopt policies that appeal to moderates, and to use public diplomacy more effectively to explain our common interests. We need a better strategy for wielding our soft power. We will have to better to combine hard and

---

[111] Nye. 42-72.

soft power if we wish to meet the new challenges."[112]   This is not to suggest that soft power is the silver bullet that will eradicate all terrorism. However, employing soft power in the right environment in subtle ways along with hard power capabilities may deter those who are susceptible to join radical groups.

F.   SOFT POWER AND NOÖPOLITIK APPLICATION IN COIN

In order to address the underlying conditions that foster terrorism, it is important to fully understand the environment that fosters terrorist activities. In Basilan, the ASG was able to gain support of the population by applying both soft and hard power tactics. The group has carried out bombings, kidnappings, assassinations, and beheadings for what they claim as their fight for an independent Islamic state in western Mindanao and the Sulu Archipelago. Their methods may create fear among the Filipinos, yet their cause attracts support among Moros. Their ability to appeal to those who share the same ideological goals makes it even more challenging for the predominately Christian Filipino government to apply soft power. Meanwhile, hard power practices create a wider wedge of distrust between the people and the state.

Successful COIN is best achieved through applying a full spectrum of power, delicately balanced at the right time in the right manner. In particular, soft power must be applied under conditions where the security environment and information atmosphere are stable enough to provide the room for the Philippine government to build a relationship with the broader population. In Southeast Asia, where hard power has historically been the primary means of dealing with insurgents, the U.S.'s ability to win the war on terror depends on the ability of both governments to combine efforts in a manner that levels out the hard power imbalance.

An alternative approach is found in-between two distinct forces of hard and soft power. On one side are more conventionally focused strategists and on

---

[112] Nye, 131.

the other side are the "noos"[113] minded thinkers. A balance of pitting the state against terrorists with enabling states and their partners to build mutually beneficial coalitions will be most effective where insurgents have an edge and the state seeks to gain an advantage. Mindanao, where the AFP and JTF-510 have pursued the ASG, is ripe for this alternative approach.

G. BASILAN STRATEGY PORTABILITY

Since the successful COIN campaign on Basilan, JSOTF-P commanders have not deviated from low intensity warfare that is increasingly focused on the civil reconnaissance and addressing civil vulnerabilities in the areas of operation. The AFP and the JSOTF have expanded its sphere of influence to other areas in the southern Philippines not with violence but through civic action programs. The illustration in Figure 1 is the authors' graphic representation of power targeting in the Republic of the Philippines.[114]

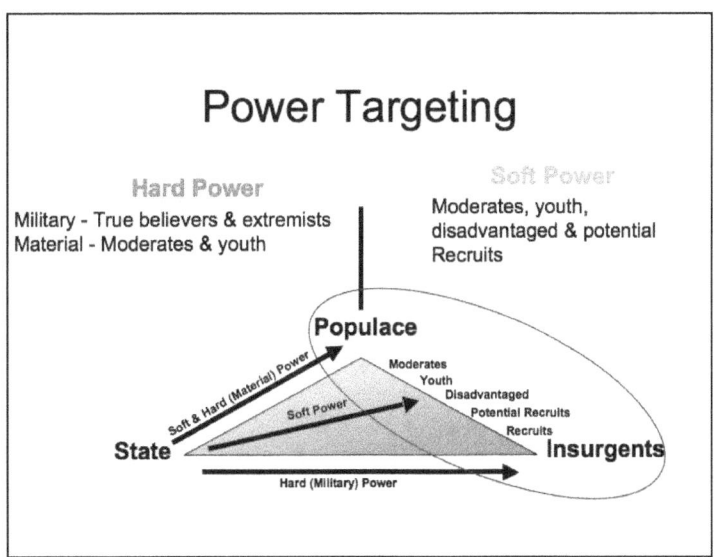

Figure 5.   Power Targeting

---

[113] John Arquilla and David Ronfeldt, "The Emergence of Noöpolitik: Toward an American Information Strategy" (Santa Monica: RAND Corporation) www.jstor.org/view/, (Accessed on February 2, 2008).

[114] Power Targeting Model adapted from Gordon McCormick's Diamond Model for COIN by Jason Smith.

Precise targeting is essential regardless of the type of power exercised by the state and its elements of national power. Since the commencement of OEF-P in 2002, the GRP and U.S. government have very accurately targeted the populace, yielding commendable results evidenced by the success on Basilan and the on-going operations on Mindanao, Tawi Tawi, and Jolo. The model listed in Figure 1 can be transposed with little modification. Of course, specific regional issues down to tribal issues must be approached differently, but the Basilan model and the Power Targeting Model can serve as templates for any insurgency. Furthermore, the distinction between an insurgency and a civil war must be recognized.

H.   U.S. STRATEGIC POLICY RECOMMENDATIONS

For nearly a half-century, the U.S. military devoted a considerable amount of effort and resources to apply soft power towards the USSR. Since the fall of the Soviet Union and the Warsaw Pact, the U.S. has scaled down significantly on its international diplomacy efforts. As a result the U.S. has yielded much of its control over the noosphere to smaller entities with fewer resources.

Exacerbating the problem, the U.S. no longer has an agency that is solely dedicated to public diplomacy. The USIA was deactivated in 1999 and reorganized under the State Department. The Under Secretary for Public Diplomacy and Public Affairs is now the proponent for strategic information and international diplomacy and has three strategic objectives:

1.   Offer people throughout the world a positive vision of hope and opportunity that is rooted in America's belief in freedom, justice, opportunity and respect for all;

2.   Isolate and marginalize the violent extremists; confront their ideology of tyranny and hate. Undermine their efforts to portray the west as in conflict with Islam by empowering mainstream voices and demonstrating respect for Muslim cultures and contributions; and

3. Foster a sense of common interests and common values between Americans and people of different countries, cultures and faiths throughout the world.[115]

The Under Secretary's objectives are congruous to the situation; however, the bureau responsible for implement the strategy, the Bureau of International Information Programs (IIP), is understaffed and under resourced, and, therefore, ill-equipped to effectively wield American soft power on behalf of the government.

Effective international diplomacy should be comprehensive and executed at all levels of the target audience. Noöpolitik is the instrument the U.S. must use to engage foreign audiences. The precise application of noöpolitik erodes extremist influences and diminishes their ability to attract and eventually recruit members. It appears that U.S. strategic information and public diplomacy will continue to lag until there is executive level emphasis placed on the program.

The U.S. government should consider reinstating the USIA as an autonomous agency and adequately equip and fund the agency so that it can achieve its stated objectives. The agency's objectives should focus on the original goals of the agency but be tailored to address contemporary audiences. Additionally, special consideration must be given to demographics that are particularly vulnerable to terrorist recruiting. By reestablishing a powerful presence in the noosphere, the U.S. can counter extremist ideology, mitigating terrorist threats. Furthermore, U.S. efforts directed toward studying the conditions before the insurgency, understanding the political environment as the insurgency grows, and executing an indirect strategy that recognizes the sensitivities and complexities of dealing with radical Islamic groups will offer a more likely victory with minimal hard power expended.

---

[115] U.S. Department of State, http://www.state.gov/r/ (Accessed on 19 March 2008).

THIS PAGE INTENTIONALLY LEFT BLANK

LIST OF REFERENCES

Abubakar, Carmen A., "Islam in the Philippines,"
http://www.ncca.gov.ph/about_cultarts/comarticles.php?artcl_Id=232
(Accessed on 25 March 2008).

Abuza, ZacharyZ, *Militant Islam in Southeast Asia* (Boulder, Lynne Rienner Publishers, 2003).

"Al Qaeda Suspect Sentenced: 12 Years in Philippines Prison for Indonesian Man with Terror Links" *CBS News,* April 18, 2002,
http://www.cbsnews.com/stories/2002/04/18/terror/main506549.shtml
(Accessed on February 2, 2008).

Arquilla, John and David Ronfeldt, "The Emergence of Noöpolitik: Toward an American Information Strategy" (Santa Monica: RAND Corporation)
www.jstor.org/view/ (Accessed on 2 February 2008).

Arquilla, John and Ronfeldt, David, "The Promise of Noöpolitik" *First Monday*,
http://www.firstmonday.org/issues/issue12_8/ronfeldt/index.html
(Accessed on 11 November 2007).

Bara, Hannbal, "The History of the Muslims in the Philippines,"
http://www.ncca.gov.ph/about_cultarts/comarticles.php?artcl_Id=232
(Accessed 28 June 2008).

Bates Treaty, http://www.msc.edu.ph/centennial/ba990820.html, The Statutes At Large of the United States of America from March 1897 to March 1899 and Recent Treaties, Conventions, Executive Proclamations, and The Concurrent Resolutions of the Two Houses of Congress, Volume XXX, published by the U.S. Government Printing Office, 1899. Copy courtesy of the U.S. Library of Congress, Asian Division (Accessed on 30 September 2008).

Bohorquez, Tysha, *"Soft Power -The Means to Success in World Politics,"* December 2005, UCLA International Institute, Tysha Bohorquez reviews Joseph Nye Jr.'s book on the importance of soft power,
http://www.international.ucla.edu/article.asp?parentid=34734 (Accessed on 27 April 2008).

Burnham, Gracia, *In the Presence of My Enemies*, (Wheaton, Illinois, Tyndale House Publishers, Inc, 2003).

Castro, Delfin, Major General (Retired), Philippine Army, "A Mindanao Story: Troubled Decades in the Eye of the Storm." Philippines, 2004.

Chalk, Peter, "Militant Islam Extremism in the Southern Philippines" in Jason F. Isaacson and Colin Rubinstein (editors), *Islam in Asia: Changing Political Realities* (New Brunswick and London: Transaction, 2002).

Country Reports on Terrorism Released by the Office of Coordinator for Counterterrorism, *U.S. Department of State*, April 30, 2007, http://www.state.gov/ct/rls/crt/2006/82731.htm (Accessed on 4 July 2008).

Cuerpo, Jose Maria III, Major, Philippine Army, interview on 11 November 2007.

Davis, Paul K. and Jenkins, Brian Michael "Deterrence and Influence in Counterterrorism" (Santa Monica, RAND Corporation, 2002), http://www.rand.org/pubs/monograph_reports/MR1619 (Accessed on 9 May 2008).

Dionco, Cecilia, Noble Director of Office of STRATCOM February 8, 2004 1st Barangay Counterterrorism Council Meeting.

Dolan, Ronald, ed. *"Philippines: A Country Study,"* (Washington: GPO for the Library of Congress, 1991).

Eduarte, Michelle, Philippine Government employee in the Department of Foreign Affairs; American Affairs,and a member of the VFA commission.

Global Security, http://www.globalsecurity.org/security/profiles/fathur_rahman_al-ghozi.htm (Acessed on July 21, 2008).

Hart, Basil Liddell, *Strategy* (New York: Penguin Group, 1991).

Hunt, Chester L., "Philippines Religious Life," Edited by Ronald E. Dolan (1991) http://www.libraryofcongress.gov (Accessed on January 28, 2008).

Hunt, Chester L., "Philippines: Social Values and Organization," Edited by Ronald E. Dolan (1991) http://www.libraryofcongress.gov (Accessed on January 28, 2008).

Hunt, Chester L., "Philippines: Muslim Filipinos" Edited by Ronald E. Dolan (1991) http://www.libraryofcongress.gov (Accessed on January 28, 2008).

Internet World Stats, http://www.internetworldstats.com/asia/ph.htm (Accessed on 24 September 08).

Islam Online, http://www.islamonline.net/English/views/2001/12/article8.shtml. (Accessed on 10 March 2008).

Juergensmeyer, Mark, *Terror in the Mind of God,* 3rd ed. (Berkeley: University of California Press, 2003).

Kenney, Kristie, U.S. Ambassador to the Philippines, July 21, 2007, "Remarks Commemoration for Victims and Heroes of Terrorism Malacanang Palace", http://manila.usembassy.gov/wwwhs236.html (Accessed on February 17, 2008).

Kohut, Andrew and Stokes, Bruce, *America Against the World: How We Are Different and Why We Are Disliked* (New York: Times Books, 2006). www.pewresearchcenter.org (Accessed on January 28, 2008).

Krepinevich, Andrew F., *The Army and Vietnam* (Baltimore, Maryland: The Johns Hopkins University Press, 1986).

Krepinevich, Andrew F., "How to Win in Iraq," *Foreign Affairs*, http://www.foreignaffairs.org/20050901faessay84508/andrew-f-krepinevich-jr/how-to-win-in-iraq.html (Accessed on 2 February 2008).

Kull, Steven, "America's Image in the World," March 04, 2007, Testimony before House Committee on Foreign Affairs, Subcommittee on International Organizations, Human Rights, and Oversight: http://www.worldopinion.org (Accessed on 21 January 2008).

Lawrence, Bruce B., "The Eastward Journey of Muslim Kingship," *Oxford History of Islam*, John Esposito ed. (New York: Oxford University Press, 1999).

Majul, Cesar Adib, The Moro Struggle in the Philippines," *Third World Quarterly* 10, no. 2, (1988), 910.

Marlay, Ross, "Philippines Regional Autonomy," Edited by Ronald E. Dolan (1991) http://www.libraryofcongress.gov (Accessed on January 28, 2008).

Marlay, Ross, "Philippines: Relations with the United States" Edited by Ronald E. Dolan (1991) http://www.libraryofcongress.gov (Accessed on January 28, 2008).

McAdam, Doug, *Political Process and the Development of Black Insurgency, 1930-1970*, (The University of Chicago Press, Chicago, 1999).

McCormick, Gordon, Gordon McCormick is the Department Chair for Defense Analysis at the Naval Postgraduate School. His "Diamond Model" for counterinsurgency is a theoretical illustration that laid the conceptual groundwork incorporated in counterinsurgency strategy of OEF-P, which was written about by Colonel Gregory Wilson in, *Anatomy of a Successful COIN Operations: OEF-Philippines and the Indirect Approach, p. 4*

Millard, Mike *Jihad in Paradise: Islam and Politics in Southeast Asia* (New York: M.E. Sharpe, Inc., 2004).

Miller, Allen G., "Philippines: Counterinsurgency Campaign," Edited by Ronald E. Dolan (1991) http://www.libraryofcongress.gov (Accessed on January 28, 2008).

Miller, Allen G., "Philippines: The Counterinsurgency Campaign," Edited by Ronald E. Dolan (1991) http://www.libraryofcongress.gov (Accessed on January 28, 2008).

Nye, Joseph, *"Politics in an information age is not only about whose military wins but whose story wins,"* February/March 2005, Boston Review, http://www.bostonreview.net/BR30.1/nye.html (Accessed on 27 April 2008)

Nye, Joseph, *Soft Power* (New York: Public Affairs, 2004).

Nye, Joseph S. "Soft Power and Leadership," http://www.hks.harvard.edu/leadership/Pdf/SoftPowerandLeadership.pdf (Accessed on 29 January 2008).

Nye, Joseph S. "The Benefits of Soft Power," August 2, 2004: http://hbswk.hbs.edu/archieve/4290.html// (Accessed on 20 January 2008).

Nye, Joseph S., *Soft Power. The Means to Success in World Politics* (New York: Public Affairs, 2004), 28.

Nye, Joseph S. "The Benefits of Soft Power," August 2, 2004: http://hbswk.hbs.edu/archieve/4290.html// (Accessed on 20 January 2008).

Philippine Presidential Commission on the Visiting Forces (VFACOM).

Porcalla, Delon, "2 Dead in the Batasan blast: Akbar, Driver Killed, and 12 hurt", *The Philippine Star*, 14 November 2007, Vol. XXII, No. 109, sec. A.

Radio Free Europe Radio Liberty, www.rferl.org/content/article/1073305.html (Accessed on 28 September 2008).

Ressa, Maria, "Passport to Terrorism" *CBS News Online Indepth,* http://www.cbc.ca/news/background/jabarah (Accessed on 11 June 2007).

Ressa, Maria, *Seeds of Terror* (New York: The Free Press, 2003).

Reuters, "U.S. War Costs in Iraq Up – Budget Report," Jan 23, 2008: http://www.reuters.com/article/asiaCrisis/idUSN23650654 (Accessed on 20 January 2008).

"Rewards for Justice Pays $10 Million in Philippines; $5 Million Reward Each Paid for Two Abu Sayyaf Terrorist Leaders" (June 7, 2007), Rewards for Justice, http://www.rewardsforjustice.net/index/cfm?page=p_payout&language=English (Accessed on 10 March 2008).

Rodell, Paul A., "The Philippines and the Challenge of Transnational Terrorism," *Terrorism and Violence in Southeast Asia: Transnational Challenges to States and Regional Stability*, Paul J. Smith ed., (New York: M.E. Sharpe, Inc., 2005).

"RP-U.S. Enhanced Cooperation on the War on Terror," Memorandum Order No. 37, 2001.

Rumsfeld, Donald, U.S. Secretary of Defense, "21st Century Transformation of U.S. Armed Forces" (speech given at the National Defense University, Fort McNair, Washington D.C. on January 31, 2002), http://www.defenselink.mil/speeches/speech.aspx?speechid=183 (Accessed on 15 September 2007).

Sepp, Kalev, "Best Practices in Counterinsurgency," *Military Review*, (May-June 2005).

"Southern Philippines Backgrounder: Terrorism and the Peace Process," *International Crisis Group* (July 13th, 2004).

Stone, Paul, "Cebrowski Sketches the Face of Transformation," *U.S. Department of Defense, American Forces Press Service News Articles* (December 29, 2003), http://www.defenselink.mil/news/newsarticle.aspx?id=27559 (Accessed on 23 September 2007).

Terrorism Knowledge Base, http://www.tkb.org/GroupRegionModule.jsp?countryid=RP&pagemode=group&regionid=5 (Accessed on 2 February 2008).

Tiongson, Edward, Vice President of the Liga ng Barangay.

Turbiville, Graham H. Jr.,"Bearers of the Sword: Radical Islam, Philippines Insurgency, and Regional Stability", *Military Review* (Mar-Apr 2002), http://www.smallwars.quantico.usmc.mil/search/lessonslearned/philippines/bearers.asp#end57 (Accessed on 21 January 2008).

Van Creveld, Martin, *Transformation of War* (New York: The Free Press, 1991).

Walley, Cherilyn, "A Century of Turmoil: America's Relationship with the Philippines" *Special Warfare;* September 2004.

Walley, Cherilyn, "Civil Affairs: A Weapon of Peace on Basilan Island" *Special Warfare;* September 2004.

"What Does Iraq Cost? Even More Than You Think," November 18, 2007: http://www.washingtonpost.com/wpdyn/content/article/2007/11/16/AR2007 111600865.html (Accessed on 20 January 2008).

World Public Opinion.org, http://www.americansworld.org/digest/overview/us_role/multilateralism.cfm (Accessed 22 June 2008).